SAN FRAI

|CONDENSED|

 tom given

LONELY PLANET PUBLICATIONS
Melbourne • Oakland • London • Paris

GW00367962

contents

San Francisco Condensed
1st edition – October 2002

Published by
Lonely Planet Publications Pty Ltd
ABN 36 005 607 983
90 Maribyrnong St, Footscray, Vic 3011, Australia
www.lonelyplanet.com or AOL keyword: lp

Lonely Planet offices
Australia Locked Bag 1, Footscray, Vic 3011
  ☎ 613 8379 8000 fax 613 8379 8111
  |e| talk2us@lonelyplanet.com.au
USA   150 Linden St, Oakland, CA 94607
  ☎ 510 893 8555 Toll Free 800 275 8555
  fax 510 893 8572
  |e| info@lonelyplanet.com
UK   10a Spring Place, London NW5 3BH
  ☎ 020 7428 4800 fax 020 7428 4828
  |e| go@lonelyplanet.co.uk
France 1 rue du Dahomey, 75011 Paris
  ☎ 01 55 25 33 00 fax 01 55 25 33 01
  |e| bip@lonelyplanet.fr
  www.lonelyplanet.fr

Design Gerilyn Attebery Editing Suki Gear & Erin
Corrigan Maps Herman So, Laurie Mikkelson, Bart
Wright & Annette Olson Cover Emily Douglas & Maria
Vallianos Publishing Managers Diana Saad & Katrina
Browning Thanks to Gabrielle Green, Tom Downs,
James Hardy, Charles Rawlings-Way, Ruth Askevold,
Tracey Croom, Wade Fox, Valerie Sinzdak, David
Zingarelli, Andreas Schueller, Ken DellaPenta, Alison
Lyall, Rowan McKinnon & LPI

Photographs
Many of the photographs in this guide are available
for licensing from Lonely Planet Images:
www.lonelyplanetimages.com
Image also used with kind permission of the Bancroft
Library, University of California, Berkeley.

Front cover photographs
Top: Golden Gate Bridge
(John Elk III)
Bottom: Golden Gate Bridge
(Paul Simcock, Image Bank/Getty Images)

ISBN 1 74059 380 4

how to use this book

SYMBOLS

⊠	address
☎	telephone number
Ⓜ	BART & Muni light rail
🚌	nearest bus route
🚗	auto route, parking details
⊘	opening hours
ⓘ	tourist information
$	cost, entry charge
e	email/website address
♿	wheelchair access
👶	child-friendly, or age requirement
✕	on-site or nearby eatery
V	good vegetarian selection

COLOR-CODING

Each chapter has a different color code, which is reflected on the maps for quick reference (eg, all Highlights are bright yellow on the maps).

MAPS

The fold-out maps inside the front and back covers are numbered from 1 to 7. All sights and venues in the text have map references which indicate where to find them on the maps; eg, (5, F7) means Map 5, grid reference F7. Although each item is not pin-pointed on the maps, the street address is always indicated.

PRICES

Price gradings (eg, $10/5) usually indicate adult/concession entry charges to a venue. Concession prices can include senior, student, member or coupon discounts.

AUTHOR AUTHOR !

Tom Given

Tom Given came to the San Francisco Bay Area for college and never left. He moved into the city the week his classes ended and stayed, despite a serious love affair with the city of Los Angeles. (LA was sunny, warm and glamorous, but there was something about the freedom of walking and taking the Muni that made up for the fog and wind.)

Tom Given also wrote *Boston Condensed*, *Chicago Condensed* and *Washington, DC Condensed*.

Thanks to David Oakes, Eric & Kate Satz, Jim Touchstone and Patty Unterman. Special thanks to Bill Wilkinson, who has made San Francisco feel like home for over 20 years.

READER FEEDBACK

Things change – prices go up, schedules change, good places go bad and bad places improve or go bankrupt. So, if you find things better or worse, recently opened or long since closed, please tell us and help make the next edition even more accurate. Send all correspondence to the Lonely Planet office closest to you (listed on p. 2) or visit e www.lonelyplanet.com/feedback.

facts about san francisco

We love San Francisco for the same reasons we love Rio or Sydney, because she is a great beauty with a great spirit.

Her beauty is legendary. From a distance, white buildings spill down 43 hills to the blue bay dotted with sailboats and islands. Up close, there's gingerbread trim on the houses, the smells of seafoam and cooking on the wind.

Her spirit is legendary, too. Born wild in the gold rush, she's never quite been tamed. This is where sailors were shanghaied to Shanghai, where mining moguls dined with opera stars, where Communist dock workers shut down the waterfront. Beats and hippies, gays and dot-commies all came here to invent new ways of living, transforming the city and American culture in the process.

Her beauty and spirit thrive despite construction, congestion and a cost of living comparable to New York and London. From the parking lot of a Safeway store, there's the sight of the water and the Golden Gate Bridge. On a Noe Valley side street, there's a poem on the sidewalk.

These pleasures are not reserved for locals. You will need connections to lunch at the Pacific Union Club, but the basic pleasures of life here – wonderful food, sparkling nightlife and those glorious views – are there for everyone. Watch the white fog fill the Golden Gate as the sunset lights up the windows across the bay, and you might leave your heart in San Francisco too.

Mario's Bohemian Cigar Store Cafe in formerly bohemian North Beach

HISTORY

Small groups of Native Americans lived on the fog-bound peninsula between the Pacific Ocean and San Francisco Bay before a Spanish party coming over-land from Monterey spotted the bay from present-day Palo Alto in 1769.

The Spanish arrived for good in 1776, building a fort at the north tip of the peninsula and a mission on a sheltered spot in the center. The Indians moved into the mission, but eventually died off from disease. Mexican offi-cials replaced the Spanish in 1821, but little else changed until 1846, when the Americans captured the fort in a tiny sideshow of the Mexican War.

The City That Was Never a Town

In January 1847, the first US mayor renamed the settlement 'San Francisco.' A year later, John Marshall discovered gold along the American River near present-day Sacramento. By 1849, word was out across the world and the California gold rush was on. The settlement exploded, from 800 people in early 1847 to almost 100,000 in late 1849. Hundreds of abandoned ships sat in the harbor, their crews off in the goldfields. The new city was wild (ex-convicts from Sydney were only one of the gangs roaming the streets) and crude (six major fires roared through in the first few years).

A silver boom followed in 1859 when Henry Comstock discovered his lode. As gold and silver poured in, mansions like the Flood Mansion at 1000 California St went up on Nob Hill, the Palace Hotel went up downtown, and Golden Gate Park emerged from the sand dunes near the ocean. By 1900, San Francisco was the capital of the American West, the ninth-largest city in the country, with 400,000 residents.

Earthquake & Fire

At 5:12am on April 18, 1906, the great quake struck, estimated at 8.25 on the Richter scale. Hundreds, perhaps thousands, were killed by collapsing

Market and New Montgomery Sts after the quake and fire of 1906

Courtesy of the Bancroft Library

buildings. The city's water system was smashed, leaving hundreds of thousands homeless as fires burned almost everything from Mission Dolores north and east to the bay. The Mission Dolores was saved by a miracle when water appeared from a hydrant at Church and 20th Sts on the third day after the quake.

Recovery

San Francisco was rebuilt in time to celebrate the opening of the Panama Canal with the Panama-Pacific Exposition on the reclaimed marshes of the Marina District. The city retained its title as financial capital of the West but began losing ground to Los Angeles as LA boomed in the 1920s. The Great Depression hit San Francisco particularly hard, culminating in the general strike of 1934 that shut the city down for three full days.

The attack on Pearl Harbor transformed the city and the rest of California. Millions of workers came west to work in shipyards and defense plants. Millions more passed through on their way across the Pacific, promising to return

The Flood Mansion (1886) is sitting pretty.

when the war ended. The wartime boom ran almost 50 years, until the cutbacks in defense spending after the collapse of the Soviet Union.

The New Jerusalem

Not all the newcomers came for good jobs and new homes in new suburbs. San Francisco had always had a bohemian edge, but with postwar peace and prosperity, people arrived to create a new culture – a counterculture – that may prove one of the city's most lasting achievements.

Artists, musicians and writers who became known as the Beats settled around North Beach, setting new styles and creating institutions like the City Lights Press. Gay men and lesbians who had discovered their orientations in the armed forces stayed here instead of going home, creating the foundations of a community that would flower in the 1970s. Political activists in Berkeley built a student movement that would take the world by storm. In the Haight-Ashbury, hippies in tie-dye began an affair with sex, drugs and rock & roll that has outlived Richard Nixon and Jerry Garcia.

San Francisco today bears the marks of all these migrants, along with marks left by waves of immigrants who came for more conventional reasons. The dot-com boom of the 1990s may be over and the city may be broke, but San Francisco is still one of the most appealing cities in the Western world.

ORIENTATION

San Francisco covers the tip of the large peninsula that separates the Pacific Ocean from San Francisco Bay. It's compact – about 7 sq miles – running from the oldest parts of the city around the Mission Dolores and along the northeast waterfront out to the rows of little boxes that line the avenues near the ocean. Most of visitors' San Francisco – downtown, Chinatown, North Beach, the Wharf – is in the triangle north of Market St and east of Van Ness Ave. Other popular areas of San Francisco are farther out Market St – the Castro, the Mission District, Twin Peaks – and out the California St corridor – Pacific Heights, the Marina District, the Presidio. Golden Gate Park cuts a swath across the far west side of the city, from near Ashbury St to Ocean Beach.

ENVIRONMENT

San Francisco is clean by big-city standards. There's not much heavy industry, and there is a transit system that provides decent alternatives to driving. Any smog that is produced usually blows inland in the afternoon when the wind kicks in from the ocean. You can swim in the ocean if you don't mind extremely cold water, and you can also swim in the bay.

Almost all the mountains and ridges that ring San Francisco Bay are protected as local, state or national parks, including the set of parks that run up the coast from the Golden Gate to Point Reyes. There is hardly any place in the Bay Area more than 30 minutes from open spaces.

With all this bounty, it's no accident the city is a center of environmental consciousness. The Sierra Club was founded here in 1892 and still calls San Francisco home. The prevailing slow-growth attitude costs San Franciscans time and money, especially reflected in the cost of housing, but they are generally happy to pay the price.

Where's the smog? The wind blows the pollutants over to towns farther inland.

GOVERNMENT & POLITICS

In politics as in life, San Francisco marches to its own beat. The city and county is run by the Board of Supervisors, elected from 11 small districts, which allows almost anyone to enter politics. Local officials range from liberal (as in 'just a liberal') to quite left wing ('progressive' in local parlance). The results are sometimes endearing – the city requires companies that do business with the city to provide domestic partner benefits for their unmarried employees – and sometimes infuriating – the city spends $1 million a year to pick up, store and clean shopping carts abandoned by homeless people, 90% of which are never retrieved by their owners.

The best that one can say of the situation is San Franciscans genuinely care about their neighbors when residents of other large US cities just want a rebate on their taxes and the homeless off the streets. The worst that one can say is San Franciscans consistently confuse good intentions with good policies, providing right-wing radio talk show hosts with great material.

Did You Know?
- The median price of a single family home is $549,000.
- A one-bedroom apartment in a nice neighborhood will cost about $1,800 a month.
- The University of California Medical Center is the largest single employer in the city.
- There are nine jobs in San Francisco for every seven residents.

Anthony Pidgeon

City workers on Post St near Union Square

ECONOMY

San Francisco is still a major financial center, even if it's no longer the capital of the American West. Twenty-two banks have headquarters here at last count, and an extraordinary number of investment bankers and venture capitalists are based from here south to Menlo Park and Palo Alto. The money people are here because the Bay Area has been one of the greatest – if not the greatest – technology incubator in the world for the past 50 years. Most of the tech work and almost all the manufacturing actually happens in the South Bay and East Bay suburbs.

Tourism is the single biggest business inside city limits. More than 16 million people visit San Francisco every year, staying an average of $4\frac{1}{2}$ days and spending an average of $123 each day.

SOCIETY & CULTURE

Thirty years ago, San Francisco was a white, heavily Irish and Italian community with good-sized Asian, Latino and African American minorities. Today, it's the most cosmopolitan small town on Earth. According to the 2000 census, 43% of the population is non-Latino white, 30% is

Asian, 7% is black. More than 10% classify themselves as 'other.' In addition, best estimates say at least 11% of city residents, some 80,000 people, are gays or lesbians.

All these different people live together remarkably well. Although San Franciscans tend to live and socialize among their own kind (like people everywhere), they also tend to live next door to many other kinds of people. This constant proximity to strangers, and the almost aggressively easygoing attitude, encourages a kind of public civility that masks many surviving prejudices.

Above a certain income level and below a certain age level, questions of origins and orientations already take a back seat

Chinese chess in Portsmouth Square

to questions of personal interests and social class. As commercial rents and housing continue to rise (nine of the 10 least-affordable housing markets in the US are in Northern California), the critical question is whether the rising tide of gentrification will lift all boats for San Franciscans, even those without real estate or rent-controlled apartments.

Etiquette

San Franciscans are serious about being laid-back. It's impolite to push, in traffic or in line. They are also serious about giving one another space. Don't smoke anywhere indoors. Don't park in front of someone's driveway without permission.

The world headquarters of Levi's, Gap and Esprit is easygoing about dress. However, expect a measure of formality (sport coat, maybe even a tie for men; skirt, dress or good slacks for women) at some restaurants, the symphony, the opera or the theater.

San Franciscans often drive carelessly. Watch yourself whether you're on foot or behind the wheel.

ARTS

San Francisco's relationship to the arts reflects her hedonistic gold-rush background. Where Boston or Chicago support the arts out of virtue, San Francisco supports the arts out of pleasure. There's a broad range of cultural activity here, but little of that earnest 'eat-your-veggies' attitude.

Music

Music has dominated the art scene since the first concert halls went up in the gold rush. San Franciscans have always spent money for first-rate opera (Enrico Caruso was on tour here when the quake struck in 1906). They also support a first-rate symphony, led by Michael Tilson Thomas. There are smaller opera companies, musical ensembles and music schools to supplement the big companies, from the Western Opera Company, which works the smaller venues of the region, to the Kronos Quartet, which works the whole world.

Popular music is an even bigger deal here than the classical kind. Long before the 1960s and folk singers and 'sex, drugs and rock & roll,' San Francisco was known for nightclubs and jazz joints. Jerry Garcia is ungratefully dead, but the city is still home or home-away-from-home to musicians from Neil Young to Counting Crows, with venues for all kinds of music from small clubs in the Mission to larger venues like the Fillmore.

Theater

San Francisco has a small but serious theater scene, dominated by the repertory companies at American Conservatory Theater downtown and

The War Memorial Opera House, serving the high brow since 1932

the Berkeley Repertory Theater in Berkeley. The Best of Broadway series presents national touring companies at the Curran and Golden Gate Theaters, and smaller theaters dot the Mission District and the area around Union Square.

Dance

The San Francisco Ballet is the oldest professional ballet company in the USA, founded in 1933 as an adjunct to the San Francisco Opera and spun off into an independent organization in 1942. Ballet season runs February through May.

A dozen other ballet companies, a dozen other dance troupes and a dozen more modern dance organizations make the Bay Area home. Visitors can catch their work at their studios, at performance spaces in San Francisco and Oakland, and at suburban venues including the Zellerbach Auditorium at UC Berkeley, Dinkelspiel Auditorium at Stanford, the Marin Center and the Dean Lesher Center in Walnut Creek.

Art

San Francisco has a funny relationship with the visual arts. The city is artist-friendly, from the large number of art schools and institutes to the risk-taking, 'no rules' ambience, but it is not artist-crazy. It's probably the competition from the physical beauty of the city and landscape: San Franciscans looking for visual stimulation tend to go outdoors rather than in.

If you do venture indoors, you will find good work by local artists and good work from all over in local museums and galleries. Painting and photography are particularly well-represented. Local icons of the 20th century like Wayne Thiebaud, Imogene Cunningham and Ansel Adams share the spotlight with contemporary locals like artist Nathan Oliveira and photographer Richard Misrach.

Literature

The city's relationship with the written word is as complicated as its relationship with the visual arts. San Franciscans do read, at least in comparison to their neighbors in LA or San Diego, but they're more likely to know the name of a local author than they are to know her work.

Since Mark Twain got his start here as a reporter during the gold rush, outsiders have chronicled the lives of other outsiders, from Jack London to Jack Kerouac. Current writers like Amy Tan and Chitra Banerjee Divakaruni follow that tradition. What's missing is a tradition of stories about the city itself. Armistead Maupin's *Tales of the City* books, which began as a daily column in the *San Francisco Chronicle*, are the exception that proves the rule. Perhaps there's not enough history here, or enough shared history of the different groups that call San Francisco home.

highlights

The highlights of San Francisco reflect her beauty an[d] outdoor spaces are everywhere. Some are places to l[ook out, like Twin] Peaks or the Embarcadero. Others look inward, like th[e gardens] of Golden Gate Park and the gardens of Yerba Buena Center. Wonderful neighborhoods are everywhere, too. Chinatown meets North Beach, the Castro slides into the Mission, each neighborhood bearing the sounds, sights and smells of a distinct way of life.

Most of these highlights are easy to get to on Muni or on foot if you have good shoes and decent blood pressure. Riding and walking are the best ways to put the sights in context and to notice details you'd miss when driving. Get a Muni Passport (p. 111) to save yourself the search for exact change. Then get yourself some water and go.

Summer winds will chill you to the bone.

Anthony Pidgeon

Stopping Over?

One Day Explore the stores around Union Square, then lunch in Chinatown. Walk through North Beach to Fisherman's Wharf, then take the historic F line streetcar along the Embarcadero to the Castro for coffee. Dine South of Market; stay there for some clubbing.

Two Days Spend the morning in Golden Gate Park. Lunch at the Beach Chalet or in the Richmond District. Visit the Palace of the Legion of Honor and the Golden Gate Bridge, then do a little window shopping along Fillmore St or in the Japan Center before dinner in the neighborhood.

Three Days Visit Alcatraz if you can get a reservation, or the Museum of Modern Art and the Yerba Buena Center if you can't. Lunch in the Financial District, then take BART or the Muni to 16th St and explore Valencia St from 16th to 24th Sts. Eat in the Civic Center/Hayes Valley area, then take in a show at the Opera House, Symphony Hall, Herbst Theater or Opera Plaza. Go for drinks afterward in the Mission or the Castro.

Vigilantes
Law and order were in short supply during the gold rush. In 1851 a Committee of Vigilance formed to punish criminals. In 1856 a second committee formed after the brazen murder of a crusading newspaper editor by a city supervisor. The Vigilantes took control of the city and hanged the supervisor and another infamous killer. They held the city for three months before negotiating a turnover to the US Army.

ALCATRAZ (3, A7)

The most infamous prison in the US sits on an island in the middle of San Francisco Bay, just a mile off Fisherman's Wharf.

Alcatraz was a derelict military installation in the 1920s, when the Federal Bureau of Prisons decided to open a maximum-security prison for the toughest cons, to get those cons out of other facilities and to show the American public it was serious about fighting crime. Once it opened for business in 1933, 'the Rock' served its public relations goals even better than its primary goal of housing the most hardened criminals. The forbidding sight of the cellblock complex, clearly visible across the water in San Francisco, served as a chilling reminder to potential lawbreakers long after the prison closed in 1962.

The cellblock was originally built to house 336 but usually held between 260 and 275 prisoners, each in his own tiny cell on one of three stories. One row of the cellblock was reserved for solitary confinement (including four cells with solid steel walls, known to movie buffs as 'the hole'), but this was no Devil's Island. The Bureau used a combination of decent food, decent space and tight security to keep order, and this generally worked. Only three inmates ever escaped from the cellblock, in 1962, and it's unlikely that those three actually reached the mainland.

INFORMATION

- ☎ 705-5444
- e www.blueandgold fleet.com
- Ⓜ Muni F line
- 🚌 15, 47
- 🕐 depart Pier 41 9:15am-2:30pm, Sat & Sun 9:30am-2:30pm, Thurs-Sun 4:20pm
- 💲 day tours $13/8-12, evening tours $21/12-18, children under 5 free
- ℹ advance reservations available and usually required; prices quoted include audio cassette tour; free video at theater near dock every 30 minutes
- ♿ yes
- ✗ In-N-Out Burger (p. 83)

Anthony Pidgeon

Indian Territory

In 1969, a group of Native Americans occupied the abandoned island, claiming the rock for 'Indians of All Tribes.' They held the island for almost two years, drawing attention to their cause as legions of journalists, celebrities, antiwar activists and average people made the trip over. A number of buildings were burned (intentionally or accidentally) and still others vandalized during the occupation. Federal marshals removed the last protestors in 1971, paving the way for conversion of the island into a national park.

INDIANS WELCOME

UNITED STATES PENITENTIARY
ALCATRAZ ISLAND / AREA 12 ACRES
1 1/4 MILES TO TRANSPORT DOCK
ONLY GOVERNMENT BOATS PERMITTED
OTHERS MUST KEEP OFF 200 YARDS
NO ONE ALLOWED ASHORE
WITHOUT A PASS

Anthony Pidgeon

CABLE CARS   (5, K4 & G7)

People love cable cars for the same reasons people love San Francisco. Cable cars take the everyday – in this case, city transport – and make the everyday fun. From the standing room along the sides (best seat in the house, if you're lucky enough to snag one) the world slides by at 9mph as your wooden car climbs up and down the hills above the heart of town. There's fresh air, water views, the sounds of cables and bells and the smell of burning pine (they use wooden blocks for brakes).

Cable cars were invented here in the 1870s by Andrew Hallidie, a Scottish engineer who made cables for mining companies. He figured if you could pull a bucket of ore out of a mine shaft, you could pull a streetcar full of people up a hillside. He laid out a five-block test track on Clay St, and when that succeeded, eight other lines followed around town.

The city began abandoning lines in the 1940s, igniting a preservation movement that ultimately saved three of the five then-remaining lines. Those three lines – the California St line from Market St to Van Ness Ave; the Powell-Mason line, running from Union Square to North Beach and Fisherman's Wharf; and the Powell-Hyde line, running from Union Square over Russian Hill to Ghirardelli Square and Aquatic Park – were completely rebuilt with federal highway money in the 1980s, preparing the system for a second century of service.

INFORMATION

- ✉ Downtown turntables at Powell & Market Sts (5, K4) and California & Market Sts (5, G7)
- ☎ 673-6864
- e www.sfmuni.com
- Ⓜ Powell or Embarcadero
- ⦿ 6am-12:30am daily
- Ⓢ $2
- ⓘ Powell St lines are very crowded in high season; stand in line at the turntable to get a seat or try the California St line from either terminus
- ✗ Sears Fine Food (p. 83)

Anthony Pidgeon

Anthony Pidgeon

Historic Streetcars

When the cable cars were closed for renovations in the 1980s, preservationists convinced Muni to run its 1950s streetcars on the F line up Market St and to borrow streetcars from other cities so visitors would have something else to ride. This experiment worked so well that Muni bought more old cars (including a streetcar named Desire) and extended the F line up the Embarcadero to Fisherman's Wharf. Today the F line is one of the best ways to see a cross section of the city, without having to brave the lines for the cable cars.

THE CASTRO   (6, C1)

The Castro is one of San Francisco's most famous neighborhoods, heart of the huge gay and lesbian community, which has made a huge mark since emerging as a community in the last 30 or 40 years.

INFORMATION

- ✉ roughly bounded by Church, 14th, Eureka & 19th Sts
- Ⓜ Muni Castro or Church
- ⓘ Cruising the Castro walking tour (☎ 550-8110) Tues-Sat 10am-2pm ($40 with lunch)
- ♿ yes
- ✗ Cafe Flore (p. 87)

Anthony Pidgeon

The Castro Theatre, no ordinary cinema

The Castro wasn't always the center of the gay community. In the first place, there weren't gay communities anywhere. In the second place, the area all around Castro St was a conventional working-class type of neighborhood – predominantly Irish and Italian, with a sprinkling of Swedes – tied to working-class pubs and parochial schools.

As families began to move out to the suburbs for space and modern conveniences, gay men drawn to San Francisco began moving in, attracted first by cheap rents and then by all those other gay men. By the mid-1970s, the streets teemed with young men in tight jeans and mustaches (the Castro clone look), and the world had a gay neighborhood.

Since those early days, the import of 'gay neighborhood' has shifted, as the Castro and other neighborhoods like it grow up (there's one in most big cities now; you might just have to go looking for it). Institutions have grown up alongside the bars, to lobby the city government or to look after the sick. The Castro neighborhood is now as much a place for culture and politics as it is a place to cruise and have a good time.

DON'T MISS
- Castro Theatre (p. 90) • A Different Light Bookstore (p. 64)
- Image Leather

CHINATOWN   (5, F4)

Chinese immigrants were pioneers in the land they called 'Gold Mountain.' Chinese prospectors worked in the goldfields, and Chinese laborers built the railroad over the Sierra Nevada. In the new city of San Francisco, the Chinese built a settlement near the docks along Dupont St (now Grant Ave) and Stockton St to the west. Chinese businessmen organized the Six Companies, benevolent associations to protect Chinese residents, still in evidence today.

By the 1860s, the Chinese were a permanent part of the landscape. The community continued to grow, despite local laws that tried to restrict them to certain jobs and neighborhoods and national laws that tried to restrict immigration. (Exclusion Acts effectively barred Chinese from immigrating from the 1880s to 1943.)

Fresh blood began arriving after US immigration laws were finally changed in the 1960s. Most of the original settlers were Cantonese speakers from the Pearl River delta in southern China. The new settlers were more diverse. Restaurants serving dishes from Hunan and Szechwan began appearing alongside dim sum restaurants. The red flag of the People's Republic began appearing (ever so rarely) alongside the red white and blue of the Republic of China.

The sights and smells of these building blocks of a Chinese America fill Chinatown today. Beyond the souvenir shops on Grant Ave, housewives poke at live chickens and fish in the markets, old men play checkers in Portsmouth Square and the scents of ginger and garlic roll out of windows at dinner time.

INFORMATION

✉ roughly bounded by Bush & California Sts on the south, Kearney St on the east, Broadway on the north & Powell St on the west

e www.sfchinatown.com

Ⓜ Powell or Montgomery

🚌 15, 30

ⓘ Chinese Culture Center, 3rd floor of the Holiday Inn opposite Portsmouth Square (☎ 986-1822)

♿ yes

🍴 Gold Mountain (644 Broadway, ☎ 296-7733)

Anthony Pidgeon

Anthony Pidgeon

DON'T MISS
- Chinese Consolidated Benevolent Building • Tien Hau Temple
- Stockton St markets • Portsmouth Square (p. 40)

FISHERMAN'S WHARF (5, B1)

Fisherman's Wharf was just too good-looking for its own good. It all started about 60 years ago when Italian fishermen from North Beach opened some restaurants to try to make a living on dry land. The restaurants and food stands selling fresh crabs off the boats became popular attractions during WWII, particularly DiMaggio's Grotto, owned by Joe and Dominic DiMaggio. (Joe sold out to Dom, but took the neon sign of a baseball player with him.) Today, the Wharf is the largest draw in town.

The carnival at the Wharf never managed to ruin its beauty. Walk past the T-shirt shops and the wax museums to the end of Taylor St, see the boats, smell the salt air, feel the wind off the water, and you'll understand what brought visitors here in the first place. If T-shirts and wax museums are your thing, you'll understand what attracts so many visitors today.

Today the Wharf covers about 10 blocks of waterfront, from the faux–New England fishing village shopping and eating mall at **Pier 39** on the east to the public fishing pier that encloses Aquatic Park on the west. Ferries to Alcatraz and Angel Island run from Pier 41, and fishing boats dock at Piers 45 and 47. The red-brick warehouses of **Ghirardelli Square** and **the Cannery** bustle with shoppers. Conga players sitting in the bleachers at Aquatic Park beat out rhythms while barkers and buskers, mimes and pedicab drivers hustle for customers.

There's shopping in the warehouses and complexes away from the waterfront as far south as Bay St. This is the home of the first Cost Plus store and the site of the first big Tower Records. Amid the stores and the parking structures are hotels and more restaurants, most built in the 1960s and '70s to cater to tourists.

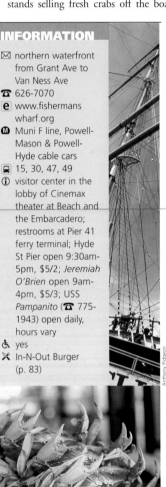

Anthony Pidgeon

Getting hungry?

Swimming Season

Members of the Dolphin Club and the South End Rowing Club swim the icy waters of Aquatic Park almost any day of the year. Both clubs are on the Hyde St Pier; both are open to the public on alternate days of the month, Tuesdays through Saturdays. Locker fees are $6.50. The clubs sponsor open-water swims throughout the year, including Golden Gate swims, swims to Alcatraz and the Escape from Alcatraz Triathalon every fall. Check [e] www.dolphin club.org and www.south-end.org, or call ☎ 441-9329 or ☎ 776-7372.

The **historic ships** at Pier 45 and the Hyde St Pier are the best attractions at the Wharf. They're open to the public year round, inside and out. Pier 45 features the USS *Pampanito*, a WWII submarine that sunk six Japanese ships in the last days of the war, and the USS *Jeremiah O'Brien*, the only surviving WWII Liberty ship in working order.

The Hyde St Pier is home to the *Balclutha*, an iron-hull square-rigger sailing ship built in Scotland in 1886 to carry grain from California to Europe around Cape Horn. When the grain trade ended, she carried lumber from Washington and Oregon down to California. The *Balclutha's* neighbors include the 1890 ferry boat *Eureka*, which used to carry cars and commuters from Hyde St over to Sausalito; the 1895 *CA Thayer*, thought to be the last commercial sailing ship to run from a West Coast port; the 1914 *Eppleton Hall*, a side-wheel tugboat; and the 1891 *Alma*, a flat-bottomed scow.

Cracked Crabs

Dungeness crabs fresh off the boats were the original lure of the Wharf. Cracked crabs and crab cocktails are still the best thing to eat here, with the possible exception of the In-N-Out burgers. Crab season runs from November to March. Crabs used to be found just outside the Golden Gate, but today most of the local catch comes from the Farallon Islands about 10 miles offshore, or from Fort Bragg and Eureka up the coast.

Anthony Pidgeon

FORT MASON CENTER (4, A3)

Fort Mason Center is a place where swords have been thoroughly beaten into plowshares. Built by the US Army in the 1860s to guard the approach to San Francisco Bay, this is the spot where millions of men and women shipped out for combat in WWII and the Korean War. Today, the fort is a cultural center managed under the auspices of the National Park Service, serving the kaleidoscope of people and interests that make up the city of San Francisco.

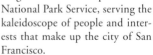

INFORMATION

- ✉ foot of Laguna St
- ☎ 441-3400
- e www.fortmason.org
- 🚌 10, 22, 30, 47, 49
- ◷ office open daily 9am-5pm
- Ⓢ free
- ⓘ visitor center for Golden Gate National Recreation Area in Bldg 201 (☎ 556-0560, recording of week's events ☎ 345-7544, box office ☎ 345-7575) open Mon-Fri 10am-4:30pm
- ♿ yes
- ✗ Greens (p. 80)

Anthony Pidgeon

The old military buildings and three huge piers house five museums and five theaters, including some of the city's best experimental playhouses. They also accommodate more than 50 nonprofit organizations – from the Oceanic Society to California Lawyers for the Arts to the Friends of Calligraphy. The list of events and classes on offer verges on a caricature of San Francisco multiculturalism. There are music classes for newborns, Zen and Tao kung fu studios, workshops on anger management and lessons in conversational Italian. There's even a gallery run the by San Francisco Museum of Modern Art where you can rent a painting or print to hang on your walls.

Each year the Fort Mason Center hosts more than 15,000 events from meetings to performances to the special events at the big piers. Local favorites include the beer festival, the wine market and the fall fashion shows benefiting local charities. Other cities may have cultural centers, but few can match the range of offerings at this little spot.

Even fewer cultural centers can match the out-of-doors attractions of Fort Mason. You can fish from the piers (you will need to bring your own bait and tackle). You can bike or hike the path that runs along the water from the Bay Bridge to the Golden Gate. Alternatively, you can enjoy a picnic on the green above the old military buildings, with its amazing views of the water, the city, Alcatraz and the Golden Gate Bridge.

DON'T MISS
- Museo Italo-Americano • Magic Theater
- SFMOMA Artists Gallery • Museum of Craft and Folk Art

GOLDEN GATE BRIDGE (3, B3)

In 1846, the American conquistador John Fremont named the entrance to San Francisco Bay 'Chrysoplae' or 'Golden Gate,' after the Golden Horn of Constantinople. The English translation stuck because the brown headlands turn gold in the sunset.

Ninety years later, an orange arc spanned the gateway, suspended by orange cables hanging from two giant orange towers on either side. It's one of the best, and certainly the biggest, art deco constructions anywhere. From the big stuff like the proportions of the 700-foot towers to the little stuff like the railings and the tollbooths, consulting architects Irving and Gertrude Morrow got the design right. They hit the bullseye with the color, dubbed 'International Orange,' which they selected to blend with the natural environment.

In contrast to most big bridges, the Golden Gate was designed as much for people as for cars. Droves of people walk the 1.7 miles every day, taking in 360 degrees of views, from the wild ocean to the city streets.

If the traffic noise on the bridge is disconcerting, or the lots at the view points are jammed, try the views from the headlands, accessible on the west side of the highway by bicycles on the weekend (bikes use the east walkway during the week) or by car (take the Alexander Ave exit north of the bridge and double back under the freeway).

INFORMATION

- ✉ Fort Point Lookout Marine Dr
- ☎ 556-1693
- e www.goldengate.org
- 🚌 29
- ⏱ pedestrian access 6am-6pm (standard time), 7am-7pm (daylight-saving time)
- 💲 pedestrians and bicyclists free, autos $3 going south
- ℹ gift shop at southeast side open Sept-May 8:30am-6:30pm, June-Aug 8:30am-7:30pm
- ♿ yes
- 🍴 Bridge Cafe, southeast side of the bridge, open Sept-May 9:30am-5pm, June-Aug 9am-7pm

Anthony Pidgeon

John Elk III

Just the Facts, Ma'am

- Length of the main span of the bridge: 4,200 feet
- Width of the bridge: 90 feet
- Height of the towers: 746 feet
- Height of the towers above the roadways: 500 feet
- Length of one cable: 7,650 feet
- Number of strands of wire on each cable: 61
- Normal speed of current in the water: 4.5-7.5 knots

GOLDEN GATE PARK (2)

The great playground of San Francisco sprawls across the western side of the city, running almost halfway across the peninsula from the Haight-Ashbury to the beach.

INFORMATION

✉ bounded by Stanyan St, Fulton St, Lincoln Way & the Great Highway

☎ 831-2700

e www.sf.ca.us/recpark

Ⓜ Muni N line

🚌 5, 7, 29, 44, 71

🕐 sunrise to sunset

$ free

ⓘ free walking tours
   ☎ 263-0991

♿ yes

✗ Park Chow (1240 9th Ave, ☎ 665-9912)

Catch your breath in Golden Gate Park.

Anthony Pidgeon

Though it's on the far side of the peninsula – a drive or a bus ride from the central parts of the city – the park is a central stage of San Francisco life. It's one of the best places to get exercise, from running and biking to roller skating and tennis playing. It's a good place to enjoy nature, from fern tree glens to formal rose gardens. It's the best place around for a picnic, on one of the meadows that line the park drives. It's also a place to see a buffalo, climb a pagoda and hit a golf ball.

All this happens in a rectangle about 3 miles long and less than 1 mile wide. That rectangle is so well designed you're rarely aware that the city is so close. Woods line the edges, and internal drives wind through the center, insulating from city noises and slowing down the city energies. All this is artificial, planted on sand dunes that used to cover the western side of the city.

At the heart of the park are the **Music Concourse** and the band shell, flanked by museums (the **California Academy of Sciences**, see p. 42, and the De Young, which is closed and about to be rebuilt). Behind the De Young lies the **Japanese Tea Garden**, a 5-acre folly built for the Midwinter Exposition in 1892 and tended by the Hagiwara family from 1895 until they were interned after Pearl Harbor in 1942 (the family also invented the fortune cookie, which became a staple of Chinese-American cooking).

The park comes alive on Sundays, when most of the east end is closed to traffic. Swarms of bicycles appear out of nowhere, along

Strybing Arboretum

This great botanical garden offers acres with thousands of plants, right in the center of the park. The sights and smells bring to mind the physical beauty of the city and its environs. The themes of the gardens, such as the native plants garden, the Garden of Fragrance for the visually impaired and the AIDS Memorial Grove, bring to mind the beauty of the city's spirit.

Refugees

The park became a city in April 1906, when hundreds of thousands of San Franciscans were burned out of their homes after the earthquake. More than 200,000 settled in here in tent cities put up by the military. Most found other places within a few weeks, but tens of thousands were stranded in their tents for months and years while the city recovered from the disaster.

with hordes of skaters and simple pedestrians. Russian immigrants from the Richmond District in their Sunday best promenade past the roller-skating disco dancers, slacker kids on skateboards and yuppie couples with kids in running strollers. The sounds of softball ring from the Great Green, and the sounds of warfare ring from the tennis courts.

To the west where cars are permitted, groups stake out picnic sites throughout the meadows that line the center drive. There may be a festival in one of the meadows or at the Polo Fields – the Hare Krishna or the farm workers or maybe an AIDS Walk. The activity eases when you get past the buffalo pens, two-thirds of the way to the windmills and the water.

There are quieter times in the park, usually on weekdays, and quieter places in the park any day of the week. Pedal boats and electric boats glide quietly around the island in the middle of **Stow Lake**. Anglers hone their fly-fishing skills at the casting pools. Nature lovers wander the fern

The Conservatory

The sugary white Conservatory of Flowers is the visual symbol of Golden Gate Park. Modeled on the greenhouse in Kew Gardens in London, it was brought over from Ireland in 1876 for mining mogul James Lick's estate on the peninsula. Lick died before it could be installed, and a group of businessmen bought it for the park instead. Badly damaged in a windstorm a few years ago, it is being renovated along its original design.

dell, the rhododendron dell and the tulip gardens at the Queen Wilhelmina windmill near the beach.

Kyoto or the Japanese Tea Garden?

Anthony Pidgeon

LINCOLN PARK   (3, D2)

Lincoln Park is a little bit of Big Sur inside San Francisco city limits. Covering the northwest tip of the peninsula, including the far corner of Land's End, it has cliffs falling into the water and secluded beaches just a short walk from a Muni stop. There are groves and meadows and wildlife, including the seals on Seal Rocks off the west end of the park.

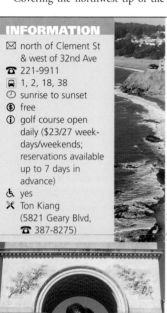

INFORMATION

- ✉ north of Clement St & west of 32nd Ave
- ☎ 221-9911
- 🚌 1, 2, 18, 38
- ⏱ sunrise to sunset
- $ free
- ℹ golf course open daily ($23/27 weekdays/weekends; reservations available up to 7 days in advance)
- ♿ yes
- ✖ Ton Kiang (5821 Geary Blvd, ☎ 387-8275)

Thinking about the Legion of Honor

The Lincoln Park Golf Course, with its views of the Golden Gate Bridge, the Marin Headlands and western San Francisco, may be the prettiest public course in the country. The **Palace of the Legion of Honor** (p. 36) next to the course is certainly one of the most elegant buildings in town. It's a three-fourths scale adaptation of the original in Paris, built by a sugar baroness who saw the design at the Panama-Pacific Exposition. A cast of Rodin's *Thinker* graces the entrance of the Palace, looking east across town.

These city parts are special, but the wild country area on the edge of the city is extraordinary. Explore this dramatic bit of the California coastline (but stay on the trails). Note that the terrain can be treacherous (trails wash down the cliff every winter), and the ocean can be deadly (people are swept off the rocks here every year).

Sutro Baths

The ruins that fill the cove at the west end of the park aren't gun emplacements from a forgotten war. They're the remains of the Sutro Baths, a Victorian amusement park that was once the world's largest natatorium. San Franciscans swam in the basins and dived in the pools here until 1966, when the baths closed – the victim of changing times. A fire in November 1966 gutted the complex, leaving the oceanfront ruins that entice visitors today.

MISSION DISTRICT   (6)

The Mission District is perhaps the most diverse, most interesting (and arguably sunniest) neighborhood in San Francisco.

The original Spanish, and then Mexican, settlement around Mission Dolores became an Anglo, mainly Irish and Italian neighborhood as San Francisco exploded in the 1850s and '60s. By 1900, the broad valley between Twin Peaks and Potrero Hill was mostly filled in, with factories to the north and east, working-class housing to the south, and middle-class homes to the west lining Guerrero and Dolores Sts.

The Mission District survived the 1906 earthquake and fire that destroyed almost everything north of 14th St. Demographic earthquakes finally changed the Mission in the 1960s. Working-class families moved out to the suburbs, replaced by Latino-American immigrants. The middle classes moved out as well, replaced by gays from the nearby Castro and straight yuppies looking for someplace sunnier than Pacific Heights. Factories eventually closed, replaced recently by lofts and dot-com offices.

The Mission today is divided in these three parts: The border between the gentry and hoi-polloi

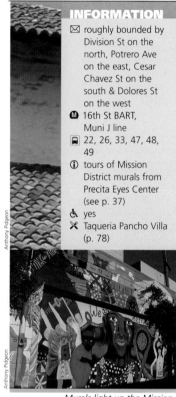

INFORMATION

- ✉ roughly bounded by Division St on the north, Potrero Ave on the east, Cesar Chavez St on the south & Dolores on the west
- Ⓜ 16th St BART, Muni J line
- 🚌 22, 26, 33, 47, 48, 49
- ⓘ tours of Mission District murals from Precita Eyes Center (see p. 37)
- ♿ yes
- ✕ Taqueria Pancho Villa (p. 78)

Murals light up the Mission.

has shifted eastward to Valencia St, with its eccentric mixture of hip boutiques, hipper restaurants, schools and commercial buildings. One block over and a few blocks south, Mission and 24th Sts are Latino-American. Spanish ads fill shop windows, Latin music blares from windows, and tropical fruits sit stacked at the markets. A few blocks east beyond Folsom St, a South of Market mix begins. Experimental theaters from the 1970s and fancy restaurants from the 1990s dot a landscape of small commercial buildings, old houses and new lofts.

DON'T MISS
- murals on Balmy Alley (p. 37) • window shopping on Valencia St
- Mission Market (22nd & Mission Sts)

MISSION DOLORES   (6, C3)

Five days before the American colonists signed the Declaration of Independence, Father Junipero Serra consecrated this site for a mission near a freshwater pond on the sheltered side of the San Francisco Peninsula.

The temporary building thrown up in 1776 was replaced six years later by the permanent structure that sits on Dolores St today. It's the oldest surviving building in the city, Landmark #1 on the official city registry. Its 4ft-thick adobe walls survived the 1906 earthquake and the fire that burned to 15th St before it was finally stopped. (Compare the 20th-century stucco buildings on the north side of 15th street with the 19th-century wood-frame buildings on the south side of the street.)

The mission was built by the local Ohlone, long gone after epidemics in 1814 and 1826, and decorated with paintings by the Indians (since restored), altar pieces from Mexico and a tabernacle door from the Philippines (another Spanish colony at the time).

The adjoining cemetery is said to house the graves of thousands of Indians from the epidemics, alongside settlers like Father Francisco Palou (biographer of Father Serra), Don Luis Antonio Arguello (first governor under the Mexicans), Don Francisco de Haro (first *alcade*, or mayor, of San Francisco) and the Noe family, whose ranch covered this area, including present-day Noe Valley.

INFORMATION

- ✉ 3321 16th St
- ☎ 621-8203
- [e] www.missiondolores .citysearch.com
- Ⓜ 16th St BART, Muni J line
- 🚌 22
- ⏱ Nov-Apr 9am-4pm, May-Oct 9am-4:30pm
- ⑤ $3/2
- ⓘ audio tour $5; Mass daily in English and Spanish, here and in the basilica next door
- ♿ yes
- ✕ Dolores Park Cafe (501 Dolores St, ☎ 621-2936)

Anthony Pidgeon

Carlotta Valdez

Fans following James Stewart and Kim Novak's steps through the film *Vertigo* will be disappointed. The tomb of Carlotta Valdez at Mission Dolores was only a prop. However, many other sites from *Vertigo* are still around for the viewing, including the shoreline near Fort Point where Novak jumped into the water, the California cable car stop in front of the Fairmont on Nob Hill and the York Hotel.

Anthony Pidgeon

PACIFIC BELL PARK (5, M9)

Not every sight in San Francisco is an artifact from the past. Pac Bell Park is a smart new stadium that starts with the scale of an old-fashioned ballpark, adds the bells and whistles of modern life, and presents the finished package in a waterfront location.

Like most major-league ballparks built since Baltimore debuted with Camden Yards, Pac Bell Park is small (about 41,000 seats) and intimate (the seats are steeply banked, close to the field). The retro brick facade along the street sides of the stadium brings to mind the ballparks of yesteryear and the old warehouses nearby.

Under the early-20th-century skin beats the heart of a 21st-century stadium. Electronic ticket systems speed spectators to their seats. Electronic vending systems speed food and drink too. Punch in an order for anything from hot dogs to sushi, and it's on its way.

This sweet space stands with its back to the winds and its face to the bay, looking across the China Basin Channel to the Bay Bridge, Oakland and the East Bay hills. The ballpark logo is a baseball splashing into the water, and baseballs really do fly there – so often that boaters cruise back and forth in the channel waiting for home runs like kids in the bleachers.

INFORMATION

- ✉ 24 Willie Mays Plaza, btw 2nd & 3rd Sts
- ☎ 972-2400
- e www.sfgiants.com
- Ⓜ Muni F line
- 🚌 10, 15, 30, 45
- 🕐 hourly tours 10am-2pm nongame days, 10am-1pm night-game days
- $ $10/5-8
- ⓘ Fan Lot kid's area (p. 43) open 2 hours before game; open nongame days Sept-May Thurs-Sun 11am-5pm, June-Aug daily 11am-5pm; no charge on nongame days
- ♿ yes
- ✕ Town's End (p. 82)

Bleacher Bums

If you want to catch a glimpse of a Giants game, there is a free standing-room section accessible from the waterfront promenade that runs behind the right-field fence. It is built right into the right field wall and offers an unobstructed view at ground level.

THE PRESIDIO (3, C5)

When the Spanish arrived here in 1776, the army occupied the northern tip of the peninsula overlooking the Golden Gate so they could control access to the bay. They built a camp, or presidio, in the lee of the hills near the fresh water at what is now called Mountain Lake.

INFORMATION

☎ 561-4323
e www.nps.gov/prsf
🚌 28, 29, 43, 82X
🕐 24-7
$ free
ⓘ visitors center (Bldg 102, Montgomery St; ☎ 561-4323) open 9am-5pm daily, closed Thanksgiving, Christmas, New Year's Day
♿ yes
✖ Warming Hut (Golden Gate Promenade at Marine Dr, ☎ 561-3040)

The little fort became a Mexican military post in 1821, when Mexico won independence from Spain. It became American in 1846, when John Fremont took the post during the Mexican War. The fort remained an American military asset, ultimately headquarters of the US Sixth Army, until 1994 when it was closed and handed over to the National Park Service.

The Presidio is a most unusual park. It's enormous – 1480 acres (1.6 Central Parks), complete with houses (21 different neighborhoods), offices (3½ million sq feet in 250 buildings) and other stuff (a chapel, library and bowling alley among other things). It's filled with nature – there are marshes and forests and ocean bluffs with Kodak views. It's filled with history – visit 200 years of buildings, fortifications and a military cemetery.

Enjoy it your way. Tour it by car, walk 11 miles of hiking trails, or bike 14 miles of paved trails. Take in the views of the bridge and the water and the Marin Headlands. Or take it easy with a lecture or a concert or a snack at the Officer's Club.

Outdoorsy types flock to the Presidio.

DON'T MISS
• windsurfers at Crissy Field Beach • gun batteries at Fort Point
• performances at the Main Post Chapel

TELEGRAPH HILL   (5, D4)

A 10-minute walk from the Financial District, Telegraph Hill may be the most charming part of this most charming city. It's not easy to get around – the streets are steep and parking is impossible – but Telegraph Hill's inaccessibility is one of its many charms.

Anthony Pidgeon

INFORMATION

⊠ bounded by Broadway, Grant Ave, Chestnut St & Sansome St

🚍 39

🕐 Coit Tower open Oct-Mar 10am-6pm, Apr-Sept 10am-7:30pm

⑤ free

✕ Malvina (1600 Stockton St, ☎ 391-1290)

This was an inconvenient part of North Beach before artists arrived in the early 20th century, drawn by cheap rent, good food and great views. By 1936, the *New York Times* was already predicting the demise of the bohemian quarter. Most of the artists are gone, finally, but their sensibility remains.

Coit Tower crowns the top of the hill. This 180-foot concrete tower shaped like a fire hose is a monument to the firefighters of San Francisco. The tower was given by a local heiress, Lila Coit, who liked chasing fire engines. (This is not an uncommon trait. When now–US Senator Dianne Feinstein was mayor, she was known to enjoy a good fire.) The Coit Tower parking lot has a two-bridge view, from the Golden Gate to the Bay Bridge, and a sensational view of the slopes of Nob Hill and Russian Hill as they fall into North Beach.

The east side of the hill was used as quarry in the 19th century. Today, houses perch on the cliffs overlooking the water. The gardens lining the walkways running up and down the east face are a riot of color, complementing the colors of the houses.

From Union and Stockton Sts, the Muni 39 bus offers good views up Lombard St to the Coit Tower parking lot. The lot is very crowded weekends and summer. Be prepared to wait in a long line or to walk up the stairs on Filbert St between Kearny and Montgomery Sts.

Anthony Pidgeon

Beatniks

Some time in the 1950s, local gossip-meister Herb Caen called the black-garbed bohemians living on Telegraph Hill and in North Beach 'beatniks,' a play on Russia's sputnik satellite. The Beat era is long gone, but their institutions survive, including the City Lights Bookstore and the City Lights Press, publisher of Allen Ginsberg's 'Howl.'

TWIN PEAKS   (3, G5)

The most famous views in a city known for views are from the Twin Peaks, two 900-foot hills that sit smack in the center of town at the end of the Market St corridor. From the observation spot on the north peak, there's a 270-degree view, from Golden Gate Park and the ocean in the northwest across the city and the bay to Mt San Bruno in the south.

Trails climb each peak for 360-degree views that pull in Lake Merced and San Francisco State University to the southwest and the mountains where the San Andreas Fault hits the water.

All this is less than 10 minutes by car from Castro and Market Sts. It's close enough to make a quick run for the best conditions – when the fog is breaking on a summer morning, when a late spring rainstorm is blowing through or when the city lights come up any clear evening. Expect crowds in the parking lot during high season. Expect cold winds whipping in from the ocean anytime.

INFORMATION

- ⊠ Twin Peaks Blvd (reached from Portola Dr, south of the peaks)
- 🚌 37
- ⓘ telescopes at view-point 25¢; sweatshirt vendors show up during the day
- ♿ yes
- ✗ Cafe for All Seasons (150 West Portal Ave, ☎ 665-0900)

Anthony Pidgeon

From below, one of the great summertime sights of the city is the thick blanket of fog hanging on the tops of the peaks. The orange TV tower on nearby Mt Sutro pokes its head through the clouds, and wisps of fog drift down into the Castro and Noe Valley, where they melt in the warm midday sunshine.

Other Views

Some other favorite places to gawk are the corner of Union and Montgomery Sts, Ina Coolbrith Park (corner of Taylor and Vallejo Sts), Alta Plaza Park (bounded by Jackson, Steiner, Clay and Scott Sts), the corner of 21st and Sanchez Sts and the corner of Broadway and Fillmore St.

Anthony Pidgeon

Hey Dad, I see Mir! View from Twin Peaks.

YERBA BUENA CENTER   (5, K5)

After only 10 years of operation, the Yerba Buena Center rivals Union Square across Market St as the heart of midtown San Francisco. It's been a long time coming, but it turned out to be worth the wait.

Thirty years ago, the stretches of 3rd and 4th Sts south of Mission were run-down, a lot like the nasty stretches of 6th St nearby. The city cleared the zone for a convention center, generating lawsuits from housing advocates. After years of litigation, a plan emerged. The main part of what became the George Moscone Convention Center went underground on the block between Howard and Folsom, and housing for seniors went up to the south and the west amid conventional condominium buildings.

INFORMATION

- ✉ bounded by Mission, Folsom, 3rd & 4th Sts
- ☎ 978-2787
- e www.yerbabuena arts.org
- Ⓜ Powell
- ⓘ outdoor performances in the gardens May-October (☎ 543-1718 for details)
- ♿ yes
- ✗ Caffe Museo at SF MOMA (☎ 357-7000)

Now, low culture rules in the **Metreon** on 4th St, where 15 conventional theaters and an IMAX can hold 3900 moviegoers at a time. High culture reigns on 3rd St, where the **Yerba Buena Center for the Arts** presents anything from Greek tragedy to Gilbert & Sullivan in its striking theater, and shows art and performance art in its less-striking gallery (see p. 36). Across Howard St, kids flock to the **Zeum**, the ice rink and the carousel.

In between, the **Yerba Buena Gardens** provide room to relax, with cafes and water features and clean green grass for a picnic or a nap. Maintained and patrolled with an eye to comfort and safety, it's the perfect chill space in the middle of town.

Just so you know, 'Yerba Buena' means 'good Yerba' in Spanish.

DON'T MISS
- Carousel from Golden Gate Park • Memorial to Martin Luther King Jr
- view from top floor of the Metreon • chess players in the gardens

sights & activities

Most of what's happening in San Francisco happens in the northeast corner of the peninsula, north of 24th St and east of Divisadero and Castro Sts. The historic heart of the city is now the **Financial District** and the shopping district around **Union Square**, with its mixture of visitors, older Chinese women changing buses and chic women of every background hunting for shoes. Just beyond, **Chinatown** and the old Italian precincts of **North Beach** sit between **Nob Hill**, with its hotels, clubs and socialites, **Telegraph Hill**, with its bohemians and wannabes, and **Russian Hill**, with a little bit of everything. Below Nob Hill, beyond Union Square, stretch the hard-luck blocks of the **Tenderloin,** which recall New York's Times Square before Mayor Giuliani.

South of Market (SoMa) is the home of the homeless and the hip, a mishmash of old warehouses, new loft buildings, motels and clubs. It slides into **The Mission**, the old Irish/Italian working-class land that's now largely Latino. Recently an influx of young people has transformed Valencia St and has brought valet parking to Mission St. **The Castro** is just up from the Mission, another working-class neighborhood, this one gentrified by gays and lesbians. **Noe Valley** is over the ridge, a straighter, richer, quieter version of Castro or Valencia Sts today.

Far from the Madding Crowd

When the magic of San Francisco wears out or wears you down, chill as the natives do. Great spots for relaxing include the gardens at **Yerba Buena Center**, the **Embarcadero** at the end of Broadway or behind the Ferry Building, **Justin Herman Plaza** at the foot of Market St, or the **Marina Green,** where parking is easy during the week.

Out California St lie **Pacific Heights**, **Presidio Heights** and **The Marina**, the silk-stocking districts, home to socialites and strivers; **Japantown**; the middle-class row houses of the **Richmond**; and the continually gentrified blocks of the **Western Addition**.

Anthony Pidgeon

The Financial District is bustling on weekdays but empty on weekends.

NOTABLE BUILDINGS

City Hall (5, M1)

San Francisco's last City Hall collapsed in the earthquake of 1906, physical evidence of the corruption in city life. Its replacement was built to erase the old memories, with grand spaces inside and out and a dome taller than the US Capitol building, based on the Hotel des Invalides in Paris.

✉ 400 Van Ness Ave
☎ 554-6023, art exhibit line 252-2568 e www.ci.sf.ca.us/cityhall
Ⓜ Civic Center 🚌 19, 42, 47 ⏱ Mon-Fri 8am-8pm, Sat & Sun noon-4pm, free tours Mon-Fri 10am, noon, 2pm, Sat & Sun 12:30pm $ free ♿ yes

Haas-Lilienthal House (4, D4)

This Queen Anne–style home was built for William Haas in 1886 and inherited by his daughter Alice Lilienthal, who lived here until her death in 1972. A one-hour tour describes the house inside and out.

✉ 2007 Franklin St
☎ 441-3004 e www.sfheritage.org 🚌 1, 47, 49 ⏱ Wed noon-3pm, Sun 11am-4pm $ $5/3 ♿ no

Hallidie Building (5, H5)

The first glass curtain-wall building in the US (based on the first anywhere, a factory in Berlin), the Hallidie was built in 1918 and designed by Willis Polk, better known for his neoclassical and arts & crafts houses. It now houses offices.

✉ 150 Sutter St
Ⓜ Montgomery 🚌 2, 3, 4, 15, 30 $ free

New Main Library (5, M2)

The New Main is either a case of good site-sensitive design or just an example of design by committee. Its west and north facades facing the Civic Center match the classic facades of the other buildings around the square. Its east and south facades are postmodern, matching the techno grace of the interior.

✉ 100 Larkin St
☎ 557-4400
e www.sfpl.org
Ⓜ Civic Center 🚌 5, 19 ⏱ Mon 10am-6pm, Tues-Thurs 9am-8pm, Fri noon-6pm, Sat 10am-6pm, Sun noon-5pm $ free ♿ yes

Octagon House (4, C4)

Built in 1861 with eight sides to catch the sunlight, this 19th-century home is owned by the National Society of Colonial Dames and houses a collection of colonial and Federal period antiques.

✉ 2645 Gough St
☎ 441-7512 🚌 41, 45, 47, 49 ⏱ noon-3pm 2nd & 4th Thurs and 2nd Sun of month, closed Jan $ $3 ♿ no

Palace of Fine Arts (3, B5)

Designed by Bernard Maybeck for the Panama-Pacific Exposition of 1915, it was designed to decay into a ruin, but San Franciscans loved the building too much to let it go. The lagoon in the front of the Palace is a favorite spot for local wedding photographers.

✉ Palace Dr at Bay St
🚌 30 ⏱ 24-7 $ free ♿ yes

Rincon Center (5, G8)

This art deco building was the main post office for 50 years. Twenty-nine Depression-style murals in the lobby depict the history of California. The atrium in the center, created when the building was renovated in the 1980s, updates the story with murals of late-20th-century California life.

✉ 101 Mission St
☎ 777-4100
Ⓜ Embarcadero, Muni F line 🚌 1, 14, 41 ⏱ 24-7 $ free ♿ yes

Anthony Pidgeon

Palace of Fine Arts

Spreckels Mansion (4, D4)

Sugar baron Adolph Spreckels (whose wife Alma gave the Palace of the Legion of Honor to the city in the 1920s) built this palace on one of the best sites overlooking the bay. It's now the private home of romance novelist Danielle Steele.

✉ 2080 Washington St
🚌 1, 12

Transamerica Pyramid (5, F5)

San Francisco's tallest building is hard to miss. At 853 feet, the 48-story structure

The Painted Ladies pose for the camera once again (at Alamo Square; see p.40).

Anthony Pidgeon

has a distinctive spire, containing the mechanical equipment. The building was completed in 1972 and nicknamed 'Pereira's Prick' (no longer in usage), after architect William Pereira. Before September 11, 2001, visitors were allowed to enter the lobby for a 'virtual view,' but even the lobby is closed to the public now.
✉ **600 Montgomery St** Ⓢ **free** ⑆ **yes**

Victorian Styles

For all her notable buildings, San Francisco is best known for the tens of thousands of 19th-century wooden houses that survived the earthquake and fire of 1906. You'll see them throughout the Castro, the Mission, the Haight and Pacific Heights, in four basic flavors – Italianate (simple, with flat false fronts and high cornices), Gothic revival (pointed arches and windows), Eastlake (also known as 'stick' for their tall, sticklike decoration) and Queen Anne (with turrets, balconies, bay windows and other fanciful decorations).

MUSEUMS

Berkeley Art Museum

(7, A5) The Berkeley Art Museum is a concrete brutalist take-off on the Guggenheim in New York – 11 galleries spiraling around a central court, showing everything from ancient Chinese paintings to modern sculpture.
✉ **2626 Bancroft Way, Berkeley** ☎ **510-642-0808** ⓔ **www.bampfa .berkeley.edu**
Ⓜ **Downtown Berkeley BART** 🚌 **AC Transit F bus from Transbay Terminal**
🕐 **Wed-Sun 11am-5pm (Thurs to 9pm)** Ⓢ **$6/4**
⑆ **yes**

Cable Car Museum

(5, G3) This is the barn where the cable cars come home at night. It's also the home of the engines that turn the cables that pull the cars up and over the hills. See the machinery, see the cars, and learn about everything from maintenance to safety procedures.
✉ **1201 Mason St**
☎ **474-1887** ⓔ **www .sfcablecar.com**
Ⓜ **Powell-Mason & Powell-Hyde cable cars**
🚌 **1, 30** 🕐 **June-Aug 10am-6pm, Sept-May 10am-5pm** Ⓢ **free**
⑆ **yes**

Cartoon Art Museum

(5, J6) The only museum in the world dedicated to cartoon art in all its forms, founded by cartoon enthusiasts in 1984 and put on a sound financial footing in 1987 with a grant from Charles Schulz, creator of 'Peanuts.' Enjoy changing exhibits from a collection of 6,000 works, classes and a bookstore for souvenirs.
✉ **655 Mission St**
☎ **227-8666** ⓔ
www.cartoonart.org
Ⓜ **Montgomery** 🚌 **7, 6, 14, 15, 21, 66, 71**
🕐 **11am-6pm (closed Mon)** Ⓢ **$5/2-3, children under 5 free** ⑆ **yes**

Chinese Historical Society Museum

(5, G4) The history of the Chinese in San Francisco is displayed in the old Chinese YWCA designed by Julia Morgan (the Berkeley architect who built the castle for William Randolph Hearst). Docent tours of the neighborhood run from the museum from time to time.
✉ **965 Clay St** ☎ **391-1188** e **www.chsa.org** Ⓜ **Powell-Mason & Powell-Hyde cable cars** 🚌 **1, 30** 🕐 **Tues-Fri 11am-4pm, Sat & Sun noon-4pm** $ **$3/1-2, children under 6 free** ♿ **yes**

Magnes Museum

(5, G8) This museum presents changing exhibits about Jewish culture and life in a variety of media. In late 2003 it will move to much larger quarters in the former Pacific Gas & Electric substation across from Yerba Buena Center, an early-20th-century building remodeled around the shape of Hebrew characters for the word 'life.'
✉ **121 Steuart St** ☎ **591-8800** e **www.jmsf.org** Ⓜ **Embarcadero, Muni F line** 🚌 **2, 7, 9, 14, 21, 31, 66, 71** 🕐 **Sun-Fri noon-5pm (to 7:30pm Thurs), closed Sat & major Jewish holidays** $ **$4/3, children under 12 free** ♿ **yes**

Maritime Museum

(4, A4) This is the dry-land portion of the San Francisco Maritime National Historic Park, which includes the five ships docked on the Hyde St Pier nearby (see p. 18). An art deco structure built as the bathhouse for Aquatic Park, its collection of photographs and ship models is worth a break from shopping at Ghirardelli Square across the street.
✉ **Beach & Polk Sts** ☎ **556-3002** e **www.maritime.org** Ⓜ **Powell-Hyde cable car** 🚌 **19, 30, 47, 49** 🕐 **10am-5pm** $ **free** ♿ **yes**

Oakland Museum of California

(7, K5) The only museum in the Bay Area dedicated to the history and natural history of California. The natural

Asian Art

The best collection in the city will reopen to the public in early 2003, when the Asian Art Museum moves to its new quarters in the Chung Moon Lee Center. This was the old main library building at Civic Center, remodeled by Gae Aulenti, the woman responsible for the Musee D'Orsay in Paris. Its 13,000 objects represent almost every culture in Asia and span over 6,000 years.

Art critics examine the goods at the Palace of the Legion of Honor.

The SFMOMA has both permanent collections and temporary exhibitions.

history exhibits are organized as a walk across California, from the environment of coastal tidepools to the environment of the High Sierra.
✉ **1000 Oak St, Oakland**
☎ 510-238-2200
e www.museumca.org
Ⓜ **Lake Merritt BART**
🕐 **Wed-Sat 10am-5pm, Sun noon-5pm (to 9pm 1st Fri of month)**
⑤ **$6/4, free 2nd Sun of month** ♿ yes

Palace of the Legion of Honor (2, A2)

Like the Museum of Modern Art, the Legion of Honor is a work of art in itself, a beaux arts confection overlooking Land's End and Golden Gate Bridge. The collection of ancient and European art inside is worth the trip even if you don't like the building and the setting.
✉ **34th Ave, north of Clement St** ☎ 863-3330
e www.thinker.org
🚌 **18** 🕐 **Tues-Sun**

9:30am-5pm ⑤ $8/5-6, children under 12 free ♿ yes

San Francisco Museum of Modern Art (5, J6)

The new star on the San Francisco culture horizon occupies one of the best buildings built in the city in the last 20 years. SFMOMA's collection is almost equal to the setting, getting stronger as an aggressive acquisition program proceeds.
✉ **151 3rd St** ☎ **357-4000** e www.sfmoma .org Ⓜ **Montgomery**
🚌 **14, 15, 30, 45**
🕐 **11am-5:45pm (to 8:45pm Thurs), closed Wed, 4th of July, Thanksgiving, Christmas, New Year's Day**
⑤ **$10/6-7, children under 12 free** ♿ yes

Yerba Buena Center for the Arts (5, J5)

This gallery is about new work by new artists, at times in new kinds of

media, as with the recent show 'Slowdive – Sculpture and Performance in Real Time.' Sometimes annoying, occasionally disappointing, but usually stimulating.
✉ **701 Mission St**
☎ **978-2782** e www .yerbabuenaarts.org
Ⓜ **Montgomery** 🚌 **14, 15, 30, 45** 🕐 **Tues-Sun 11am-6pm (to 8pm 1st Thurs of month)**
⑤ **$6/3** ♿ yes

Legion of Honor

PUBLIC ART

Balmy Alley (6, E5)
This is one of the open-air studios of the mural movement that hit the Mission District in the 1970s. It's lined with murals from end to end, some old and some new, all exploring the progressive themes of family values and political activism you'll see on walls all over the neighborhood.
✉ **between Folsom & Harrison Sts and 24th & 25th Sts** Ⓜ **24th St BART** 🚌 **12, 47, 68** Ⓢ **free** ♿ **yes**

Beach Chalet (2, D1)
The ground floor of this building is lined with Lucien Labault murals of life in San Francisco during the 1930s, familiar scenes of the docks and North Beach, Baker Beach and Golden Gate Park. A scale model of Golden Gate Park is an added attraction.
✉ **1000 Great Highway** ☎ **386-8439** 📧 **www.beachchalet.com** 🚌 **5** ⏰ **Sun-Thurs 9am-9:30 pm, Fri & Sat 9am-10:30pm** Ⓢ **free** ♿ **yes**

Father Hidalgo Statue (6, D3)
On September 16, 1810, a Mexican priest named Miguel Hidalgo sparked a revolt against Spain with the cry, 'Long Live Independence, Long Live America.' This statue of the George Washington of Mexico stands guard over the Mission District from the center of Dolores Park.
✉ **Mission Dolores Park** Ⓜ **Muni J line** 🚌 **33** ⏰ **sunrise-sunset** Ⓢ **free**

Precita Eyes Mural Center (3, G8)
Every Saturday and Sunday, Precita Eyes presents walking and bus tours of murals in different parts of town, one of the easiest ways to see public art around town.
✉ **2981 24th St** ☎ **285-2287** 📧 **www.precitaeyes.org** Ⓜ **24th St BART** 🚌 **12, 48** ⏰ **Tours depart at 1:30pm; call for details** Ⓢ **$8/2-5**

Sun Yat-sen Memorial (5, G5)
Benny Bufano, San Francisco's favorite sculptor of the 1930s and '40s, designed the statue of the Chinese revolutionary for this site in St Mary's Square.
✉ **St Mary's Square**

Sun Yat-sen Memorial

Ⓜ **California cable car** 🚌 **1, 15** ⏰ **sunrise-sunset** Ⓢ **free** ♿ **yes**

Vaillancourt Fountain (5, F7)
This brutal concrete construction was originally designed to mask the sights and sounds of the Embarcadero Fwy, which was torn down after the earthquake of 1989. Walk under it, into it, or around it for full sensory effect.
✉ **Justin Herman Plaza** Ⓜ **Embarcadero, Muni F line** 🚌 **1, 2, 41** ⏰ **24-7** Ⓢ **free** ♿ **yes**

Women's Building (6, C4)
Maestrapeace, a mural of famous and not-famous women by a group of seven women artists covers almost every bit of this four-story complex of offices and meeting spaces.
✉ **3542 18th St** ☎ **431-1180** 📧 **sfwctwb@aol.com** Ⓜ **16th St BART, Muni J line** 🚌 **26, 33** Ⓢ **free**

Depression Art
During the 1930s, the federal Works Progress Administration hired artists to decorate public buildings across the US, often in the mannerist style popularized by Diego Rivera and Thomas Hart Benton. San Francisco has more than its share of WPA glories, including the murals at Coit Tower (p. 29), the Rincon Center (p. 33) and the Beach Chalet (p. 37). If you can get an invitation, the City Club on Sansome St has a mural by Diego Rivera himself decorating the main staircase of the club.

GALLERIES

John Berggruen Gallery (5, H5)

One of the most famous in the city if not the state, this gallery presents a range of modern paintings, drawings and sculpture by American and European artists – some international brand names like Richard Diebenkorn and Mark di Suvero, some less well-known.

✉ 228 Grant Ave ☎ 781-4629 e www .berggruen.com Ⓜ Montgomery 🚌 2, 3, 4, 15, 30, 38 ◷ Mon-Fri 9:30am-5:30pm, Sat 10:30am-5pm Ⓢ free ♿ yes

Rena Bransten Gallery

(5, J5) Paintings and drawings by contemporary artists in a range of styles are the bread and butter here, but you can also see photographs and even video if you're lucky (like a recent show by bad-boy director John Waters).

✉ 77 Geary St ☎ 982-3292 e www .renabranstengallery.com Ⓜ Montgomery or Powell 🚌 2, 3, 4, 15, 30, 38 ◷ Tues-Fri 10:30am-5:30pm, Sat 11am-5pm Ⓢ free ♿ yes

Crown Point Press

(5, K6) Crown Point is a gallery, a print shop and a school rolled into one. Born as a print workshop in 1962, it produced its first fine-arts prints for Richard Diebenkorn and Wayne Thiebaud in 1965. Visit the gallery and the etching studios, or attend one of the summer workshops open to artists from everywhere.

✉ 20 Hawthorne Ln

☎ 974-6273 e www .crownpoint.com Ⓜ Montgomery 🚌 10, 15, 76 ◷ Tues-Sat 10am-6pm Ⓢ free ♿ yes

Fraenkel Gallery (5, J5)

This is one of the best places to see photography in the US. From historic images like Carleton Watkins landscapes to iconic images like Irving Penn portraits to up-and-comers like Tom Priola, Jeffrey Fraenkel has it all.

✉ 49 Geary St ☎ 981-2661 e www.fraenkel gallery.com Ⓜ Montgomery or Powell 🚌 2, 3, 4, 15, 30, 38 ◷ Tues-Fri 10:30am-5:30pm, Sat 11am-5pm Ⓢ free ♿ yes

Galeria de la Raza

(3, G8) At the center of the Latino cultural scene since the early 1970s, Galleria de la Raza presents work that speaks to contemporary Latino life.

✉ 2857 24th St ☎ 826-8009 e www .galeriadelaraza.org Ⓜ 24th St BART 🚌 12, 48 ◷ Tues-Sat noon-6pm Ⓢ free ♿ yes

Hackett-Freedman Gallery (5, H5)

No abstract impressionists here. Michael Hackett and Tracy Freedman focus on representational work by a broad range of American artists. You'll find approachable art at sometimes-approachable prices.

✉ 250 Sutter St ☎ 362-7152 e www .hackettfreedman gallery.com Ⓜ Montgomery 🚌 2, 3, 4, 15, 30, 38 ◷ Tues-

Fri 10:30am-5:30pm, Sat 11am-5pm Ⓢ free ♿ yes

San Francisco Art Institute (5, D2)

The Art Institute shows work by its own students and outside artists. Expect anything, from painting to sculpture to work in new technological media.

✉ 800 Chestnut St ☎ 749-4564 e www .sfai.edu Ⓜ Powell-Mason & Powell-Hyde cable cars 🚌 30 ◷ Mon-Sat 11am-6pm Ⓢ free ♿ yes

SF Camerawork (5, N3)

This nonprofit institution has showcased photography and related work by emerging and somewhat-established artists for more than 25 years. It organizes its own exhibits, presents traveling shows and also presents lectures on photography by the likes of William Wegman and Gary Winogrand.

✉ 1246 Folsom St ☎ 863-1001 e www .sfcamerawork.org 🚌 12, 19 ◷ Tues-Sat noon-5pm Ⓢ free

Southern Exposure

(3, F8) One of the first galleries to colonize the wilds of the Mission, located in the factory that became Project Artaud. Southern Exposure is still presenting work by emerging artists in its two huge spaces, along with lectures and education programs for artists and art lovers.

✉ 401 Alabama St ☎ 863-2141 e www .soex.org 🚌 10, 22, 33 ◷ 11am-5pm Ⓢ free ♿ yes

HOUSES OF WORSHIP

Grace Cathedral

(5, G3) This 20th-century version of a Gothic cathedral crowns the nob of Nob Hill. Splendid inside and out, from the copy of the Gates of Paradise from the Baptistery in Florence to the Labyrinth Walk and the stained-glass windows. Come for services, for organ recitals and other programs.

✉ **1100 California St** ☎ **749-6300** e **www .gracecathedral.org** Ⓜ **California cable car** 🚌 **1** ⏰ **services Sun 7:30am, 8:15am & 11am; call for other services & programs** ⑤ **free** ♿ **yes**

Holy Virgin Cathedral (2, B4)

The onion domes of this cathedral stand guard over the Russian community of the Richmond, settled here since the White Russians came over from Siberia. The icons, incense and relics, such as the body of St John of Shanghai and San Francisco, are like keepsakes from home.

✉ **6210 Geary Blvd** ☎ **221-3255** 🚌 **38** ⏰ **11am-1pm, also open for services 8am & 6pm** ⑤ **free**

♿ **limited (always available Sat & Sun)**

Old St Mary's Cathedral (5, G5)

The first Catholic cathedral in the city, built in 1854. Its stout brick walls survived the earthquake and fire in 1906, though the bells and altar were melted.

✉ **660 California St** ☎ **288-3800** 🚌 **1, 15, 45** ⏰ **Mon-Fri 7am-7pm, Sat 7am-4pm** ⑤ **free** ♿ **yes**

San Francisco Zen Center (4, H4)

The oldest Buddhist monastery in the US is a San Francisco institution. Come to meditate, attend a class or make soup for the homeless. Or just come to buy a book or enjoy a meal (they serve three squares a day).

✉ **300 Page St** ☎ **863-3136** e **www .sfzc.com** Ⓜ **Muni Van Ness** 🚌 **6, 7, 66, 71** ⏰ **office open Mon-Fri 9:30am-5pm, Sat 9am-noon** ⑤ **free** ♿ **yes**

St Mary's Cathedral

(4, F4) Mussolini goes to the Bauhaus with this 1960s design. The wide-angle view of Twin Peaks

Grace Cathedral

and the city from the inside is almost worth the excessive white cap on the outside.

✉ **1111 Gough St** ☎ **567-2020** 🚌 **38, 47, 49** ⏰ **Mon-Fri 6:45am-4:30pm, Sat 6:45am-6:30pm, Sun 7:15am-4:45pm** ⑤ **free** ♿ **yes**

Vedanta Temple

(4, C3) This Hindu temple on a quiet Pacific Heights side street was built in 1905. Replaced by a bigger temple nearby at 2323 Vallejo St, it is still in use for lectures and other events.

✉ **2963 Webster St** ☎ **922-2323** 🚌 **22, 41, 45** ⏰ **call ahead** ⑤ **free**

Glide Memorial Church

As the story goes, Reverend Cecil Williams asked God for help tending the needy in the Tenderloin, and God told him to do it himself. Today, Glide Memorial United Methodist Church (330 Ellis St; 5, K3; e www.glide .org) is an only-in-San Francisco institution that offers scores of programs for the neighborhood as well as Sunday high-gospel services (9am and 11am) that draw people from all over the city. Deeply moving and highly entertaining.

PARKS & PUBLIC SPACES

Alamo Square (3, E6)
The row of Victorian houses lining the east side of Alamo Square with the towers of the Financial District in the background is one of the most familiar images of San Francisco. Stop for a photo shoot of your own.
✉ **bounded by Hayes, Steiner, Fulton & Scott Sts** ☎ 831-2700 🚌 5, 21, 22, 24 ☼ sunrise-sunset ⑤ free ♿ yes

Buena Vista Park
(3, E6) Enjoy stunning views of the ocean, the city and the bridges from this steep hill separating the Castro from the Haight. Once an open-air playground for the Castro, it's much more sedate these days.
✉ **Buena Vista Way south of Haight St** ☎ 831-2700 🚌 6, 7, 43, 6, 71 ☼ sunrise-sunset ⑤ free

Ferry Plaza & Justin Herman Plaza (5, F7)
These waterfront plazas run along the inside of the Embarcadero from Mission St north to Washington St. Justin Herman Plaza is home to a portable ice rink in the winter and host to

brown-bagging office workers year round. The Ferry Plaza has a small farmers' market on Tuesday (the Saturday market returns in late 2003).
✉ **Embarcadero from Mission to Washington Sts** ☎ 831-2700 Ⓜ **Embarcadero, Muni F line** 🚌 2, 7, 14, 21, 66, 71 ☼ sunrise-sunset ⑤ free ♿ yes

Fort Funston (3, K1)
A former military preserve that retained almost-wild nature right inside city limits. Rising from low dunes in the north to 200ft-high cliffs in the south, this was a coastal battery during WWII and a Nike missile base during the Cold War.
☎ 556-8371 🚌 **Sloat Blvd to Great Hwy, left on Great Hwy to Fort Funston parking lot** ☼ 6am-9pm ⑤ free

Marina Green (4, A2)
The front lawn of the city overlooks the Golden Gate, Marin County, Angel Island and Alcatraz. A favorite space for jogging, skating, picnicking and kite flying. A great jumping off point to walk or bike the Golden Gate Promenade along the

water to the bridge.
✉ **Marina Blvd from Webster to Scott Sts** ☎ 831-2700 🚌 22 ☼ sunrise-sunset ⑤ free ♿ yes

McKinley Park (3, F9)
There are two crooked streets in the city – the block of Lombard from Hyde down to Leavenworth, which is filled with cars throughout the summer, and the stretch of Vermont from 20th to 22nd Sts, which is usually empty. Come for the view of the Mission District and Twin Peaks and for the ride.
✉ **Vermont & 20th Sts** ☎ 831-2700 🚌 **16th St to Kansas St, right on 20th St to Vermont** ☼ 24-7 ⑤ free ♿ yes

Mission Dolores Park
(6, D3) A microcosm of the city in four square blocks, this park has a playground and soccer pitch for the Latinos from the Mission, sunbathing for the gay boys from the Castro, tennis courts and picture-postcard views for everybody. Home stage of the San Francisco Mime Troupe and center stage for rallies and meetings.
✉ **bounded by 18th, Dolores, 20th & Church Sts** ☎ 831-2700 Ⓜ **Muni Church or Castro, J line** 🚌 33 ☼ sunrise-sunset ⑤ free ♿ yes

Portsmouth Square
(5, F5) This is the only open space in Chinatown, and everyone takes advantage of it. See tai chi in the morning, kids playing in

Levi Park
The latest gift from the Levi-Strauss people to the city of San Francisco is the inspired little park at their world headquarters complex below Telegraph Hill (5, D5). The main plaza has fountains and watercourses with stepping stones for children and the childlike who like to explore such things. The extension across the street has a stream wandering through a small grove of trees.

the afternoon and old men sitting around telling stories all day.
✉ **Kearny St btw Clay & Washington Sts**
☎ **831-2700**
Ⓜ **Montgomery** 🚌 **1, 15, 45** ⏲ **sunrise-sunset** 💲 **free** ♿ **yes**

Washington Square
(5, D3) The heart of North Beach, the square has Saints Peter and Paul Church to the north, the Italian-American Athletic Club to the east, and cafes and restaurants all around. Good for sunning,

even better for people watching.
✉ **bounded by Columbus Ave, Union, Stockton & Filbert Sts**
☎ **831-2700** 🚌 **15, 30, 39, 41, 45**
⏲ **sunrise-sunset**
💲 **free** ♿ **yes**

QUIRKY SAN FRANCISCO

AsiaSF (5, N3)
Any restaurant can feature gender illusionist waitresses. Some restaurants can even feature gender illusionist waitresses who dance on the bar in between orders. Only Asia SF has the waitresses serving fusion food so good you don't notice their outfits. Come for the shows (on the hour, every hour) or the dancing downstairs, but stay for the food. Reservations recommended.
✉ **201 9th St** ☎ **255-2742** 📧 **www.asiasf.com** Ⓜ **Civic Center** 🚌 **9, 14, 29, 47** ⏲ **Mon-Wed 6-10pm, Thurs-Sun 5-10pm** 💲 **free** ♿ **yes**

Beach Blanket Babylon (5, E3)
More than 30 years ago, a revue about life in San Francisco opened at the Club Fugazi, featuring costumes and headdresses that redefined camp. Creator Steve Silver has passed to the big wardrobe department in the sky, but Beach Blanket goes on.
✉ **678 Green St**
☎ **421-4222** 📧 **www.beachblanketbabylon.com** 🚌 **15, 30, 41, 45** ⏲ **Wed & Thurs 8pm, Fri & Sat 7pm & 10pm, Sun 3pm & 7pm** 💲 **$25-64 (21+)** ♿ **yes**

Beauty Bar (6, D4)
Would you like a manicure with that martini? You might just be able to get one in this Mission St beauty parlor converted to a bar where 'Beauty is your duty.' Try the Manicure and Martini Happy Hour Wednesday to Friday at 6pm (Saturday evening from 7pm).
✉ **2299 Mission St**
☎ **285-0323** 📧 **www.beautybar.com** Ⓜ **16th St BART** 🚌 **14, 33, 49** ⏲ **Mon-Fri 5pm-2am, Sat & Sun 7pm-2am** 💲 **free** ♿ **yes**

Foreign Cinema (6, D4)
This place is a cross between a fine French restaurant and a drive-in

movie, right on Mission St. They screen a film every night on the back wall of the patio, where you can eat and drink and hear the soundtrack on old drive-in speakers. Or eat and drink indoors, and lip-read the dialog (how's your Polish or your Portuguese?).
✉ **2534 Mission St**
☎ **648-7600** 📧 **www.foreigncinema.com** Ⓜ **24th St BART** 🚌 **14, 26, 49** ⏲ **Tues-Sun 5:30pm-2am** 💲 **free** ♿ **yes**

Hang Gliders (3, K1)
It's not your typical urban spectator sport, but every afternoon when the wind is up you can see hang gliders soaring above the

Artist Peter Rabbit pays homage to the city.

ocean at Fort Funston. If you've never seen someone jump off a cliff right in front of you, this is your chance.

✉ **Fort Funston**
🚌 **Skyline Dr south from Sloat Blvd toward Daly City; turn right at Fort Funston sign and follow access road to the right to the parking lot at the edge of the cliffs** ⏲ **sunrise-sunset (afternoons are best)** ⑤ **free**

The Mexican Bus
(5, K6) Take a classic American school bus, paint it up like a pickup from Oaxaca, wire it for sound, and you have a Latin nightclub on wheels, ready for dance-club tours, mural tours or private parties. Must be seen to be believed.

✉ **pick up at Chevy's, 201 3rd St** ☎ **546-3747** e **www.mexicanbus .com** Ⓜ **Montgomery** 🚌 **15, 30, 45** ⏲ **dance club tour Thurs 8pm, Fri & Sat 9:30pm** ⑤ **dance club tour $35**

Paxton Gate (6, D4)
The perfect place to buy a

Valentine's Day gift if your valentine will swoon for a lovingly mounted tarantula, a case of dead butterflies or maybe a stuffed snake. Stunning orchids, elegant garden gear and other knickknacks are also available if your valentine is on the stuffy side.

✉ **824 Valencia St** ☎ **824-1874** e **www .paxton-gate.com** Ⓜ **16th St BART** 🚌 **26, 47, 49** ⏲ **Mon-Fri noon-7pm, Sat & Sun 11am-7pm** ⑤ **free** ♿ **yes**

Pipe Dreams (2, C10)
The '60s are alive and well in the Haight, and Pipe Dreams has been alive and well here since the '60s got rolling, so to speak. The best selection of pipes and smoking gear in the city, sold by some of the nicest people in the city.

✉ **1376 Haight St** ☎ **431-3553** 🚌 **6, 7, 33, 43, 66** ⏲ **Mon-Sat 10am-7:50pm, Sun 11am-6:50pm** ⑤ **free** ♿ **yes**

Sea Lions (5, A3)
The developers of Pier 39 never imagined that

wildlife would push out the people life, but that's just what happened. A group of sea lions moved onto some of the docks on the west side of the marina, creating a genuine wildlife refuge (seal smells and all) in the middle of Fisherman's Wharf.

✉ **Pier 39** Ⓜ **Muni F line, Powell-Mason cable car** 🚌 **10, 39, 47** ⏲ **24-7** ⑤ **free** ♿ **yes**

Tonga Room (5, G3)
This bar is a little bit of Waikiki in the bottom of the Fairmount Hotel on the top of Nob Hill. Tropical music, tropical drinks and even tropical rainstorms complete with lightning and thunder, are all here for the price of a drink and a modest cover charge in the evenings when the band's on duty.

✉ **950 Mason St** ☎ **772-5278** Ⓜ **California, Powell-Mason & Powell-Hyde cable cars** 🚌 **1** ⏲ **5pm-2am, shows from 8pm nightly** ⑤ **$3 cover and one-drink minimum after 8pm** ♿ **yes**

SAN FRANCISCO FOR CHILDREN

Aquarium of the Bay (5, A3) Walk amid schools of fish through hundreds of feet of underwater tunnels for a different kind of aquarium experience. Conveniently located in the middle of all the action at Pier 39 near Fisherman's Wharf. Special programs run throughout the year.

✉ **Pier 39** ☎ **623-5300** e **www.aquarium ofthebay.com** Ⓜ **Muni**

F line, Powell-Mason cable car 🚌 **10, 15** ⏲ **Sept-May Mon-Thurs 10am-6pm, Fri-Sun 10am-7pm, June-Aug 10am-8pm** ⑤ **$13/6.50, children under 3 free, family rate $30** ♿ **yes**

California Academy of Sciences (2, D7)
This is a serious organization with eight scientific research departments, but it's best known as the

home of the Steinhardt Aquarium shark tank and the Gary Larson collection, which appeal equally to kids and their chauffeurs.

✉ **55 Concourse Dr** ☎ **750-7145** e **www .calacademy.org** 🚌 **5, 21, 44** ⏲ **Labor Day-Memorial Day 10am-5pm, Memorial Day-Labor Day 9am-6pm (1st Wed of month to 8:45pm)** ⑤ **$8.50/2-5.50, children under 3**

Babysitting

Most good-size hotels have babysitting services, often provided by staff members who want to make a little money on the side. If yours does not, call **American ChildCare Service** (☎ 285-2300; **e** www.americanchildcare.com; $15.50/hr for a family or up to three children, 4hr minimum) or **Bay Area Child Care** (☎ 650-991-7474; $11/hr for one child, 4hr minimum, agency charge of $15 per assignment includes provider's transport).

free, free 1st Wed of month ♿ yes

Exploratorium (3, B5)
One of the first science museums for kids, opened in 1969 by Dr Frank Oppenheimer, brother of the father of the A-bomb and an eminent scientist in his own right. It's still one of the best science museums for kids in the world, with more than 650 exhibits exploring science, art and human perception.
⊠ **Palace of Fine Arts**
☎ 397-5673 **e** www.exploratorium.edu
🚌 28, 30 ⏰ Labor Day-Memorial Day Tues-Sun 10am-5pm (to 9pm Wed), Memorial Day-Labor Day 10am-6pm (to 9pm Wed)
⑤ $10/6-7.50, children 4 and under free; tactile dome $14 ♿ yes

Fan Lot (5, M9)
A mini-amusement park hiding in the outfield of Pac Bell Park, featuring slides, a base race, and high-kitsch stuff like a giant baseball glove, a giant Coca-Cola bottle and a miniature of Pac Bell Park itself.
⊠ **Pacific Bell Park, 24 Willie Mays Plaza**
☎ 972-2000 **e** www.sfgiants.com ⓜ Muni F line 🚌 15, 30 ⏰ see p. 27 ⑤ free ♿ yes

Randall Museum
(2, D10) The official children's museum of the city has a petting zoo, art workshops and a model railway as its chief attractions. There's also hiking on the Corona Heights hill, with sensational views of the city and the East Bay suburbs.
⊠ **199 Museum Wy**
☎ 554-9600 **e** www.randallmuseum.org
🚌 37 ⏰ Tues-Sat 10am-5pm ⑤ free ♿ yes

Youngsters at Fan Lot

San Francisco Zoo
(3, H1) This is a zoo redesigned over the past 10 years with kids in mind. The Children's Zoo, with its prairie dog village and pet sheep and tarantulas, is always a hit, but other exhibits like the koala colony, the gorilla family and the Lion House (feeding daily at 2pm, except Monday) are hits with everyone.
⊠ **1 Zoo Rd** ☎ 753-7080 **e** www.sfzoo.org
ⓜ Muni L line 🚋 Sloat Blvd west to Zoo Rd
⏰ 10am-5pm (children's zoo 11am-4pm, June 12-Labor Day 10:30am-4:30pm) ⑤ $10/4-7 (discounts for SF residents with ID) ♿ yes

Zeum (5, K5)
This is a workshop for children to explore the intersection between technology and art, part of the kid-friendly complex on the roof of the Moscone Convention Center. See animators' studios or the video production lab. Play on the iMacs or take in a show at the theater. Zeum also hosts theater programs produced by the American Conservatory Theater.
⊠ **4th & Howard Sts**
☎ 777-2800 **e** www.zeum.org ⓜ Powell
🚌 12, 14, 30, 45
⏰ summer (June12-Labor Day) Wed-Sun 11am-5pm; winter (Labor Day-June 11) Sat & Sun, Mon holidays 11am-5pm; Easter week daily 11am-5pm
⑤ $7/5-6 ♿ yes

Whale Watching
Every fall gray whales pass the Bay Area on their way from the Bering Sea to Baja California. You can see them from the coast, or you can take one of the Oceanic Society Expeditions cruises that run Friday to Monday from Fort Mason during the fall and spring migrations (☎ 474-3385; **e** www.oceanicsociety.org; children 10 and older only).

KEEPING FIT

There are more ways to keep fit in San Francisco than just walking the hills. You can run just about anywhere, including the Embarcadero, Golden Gate Park and the Golden Gate Promenade (from the end of the Embarcadero through Fort Mason and the Presidio to Fort Point at the foot of the bridge). You can skate along the Embarcadero any time, and in Golden Gate Park on weekends. Want more? Consider biking, hiking or even swimming if you can take cold water.

Indoors, you'll find health clubs, gymnasiums and exercise studios with something for everyone. Indoor pools? Basketball? Tai chi for older women? You bet.

Bay to Breakers
This may be the only serious foot race in the world with prizes for best costume. Every May, tens of thousands of athletes in every state of dress and undress make the 7½-mile run (or walk) from the Embarcadero out Howard and Hayes Sts to Ocean Beach. It's a classic San Francisco cross between a marathon and a Mardi Gras.

Avenue Cyclery (2, D9)
Bicycling is one of the best ways to explore Golden Gate Park and the paths along the Great Highway. Avenue Cyclery at the east end of the park has all kinds of bikes for kids and adults, complete with helmets and locks.
✉ 756 Stanyan St
☎ 356-7833 🄔 www .avenuecyclery.com
Ⓜ Muni N line 🚌 6, 43
🕐 10am-6pm or 7pm ⑤ $5/hr, $25/day

Blazing Saddles (5, C2)
Bike to the bridge and the trails across the bay in Marin County from the Blazing Saddles locations in North Beach and Fisherman's Wharf. Choose from a range of mountain bikes and road bikes. Tandems and kid's bikes are also available.
✉ 1095 Columbus Ave

☎ 202-8888 🄔 www .blazingsaddlessan francisco.com
Ⓜ Powell-Mason cable car 🚌 10, 30, 47
🕐 daylight-saving time 8am-8pm, standard time Mon-Fri 8am-6pm, Sat & Sun 8am-7:15pm
⑤ $7-11/hr, $15-48/day

Club One (5, J4)
There are eight locations around town, including this one near Union Square, which features a three-lane indoor pool. If they don't have the machines or the class you're looking for here, try the mega-One at Geary and Fillmore Sts (4, F3, ☎ 749-1010).
✉ 535 Mason St
☎ 337-1010 🄔 www .clubone.com Ⓜ Powell
🚌 2, 3, 4 🕐 Mon-Fri 5:30am-10pm, Sat &

Sun 7am-7pm
⑤ $20/day ♿ yes

Embarcadero YMCA
(5, G8) The YMCA has everything for the fitness fanatic, from cardio machines and weight-training equipment to a full schedule of classes and a sensational indoor pool. Best during the day before the after-work set arrives.
✉ 169 Steuart St
☎ 957-9622 🄔 www .ymca.net Ⓜ Embarcadero, Muni F line
🚌 2, 7, 9, 14, 21, 31, 32, 66, 71 🕐 Mon-Fri 5:30am-10pm, Sat 8am-8pm, Sun 9am-6pm
⑤ $15/day (photo ID required) ♿ yes

Gold's Gym (5, P4)
If body image has become a monster of gay male big-city life, then the Gold's locations here and in the Castro (2301 Market St; 6, C2; ☎ 626-4488) are the belly of the beast. If you can stand the testosterone, you'll find first-rate facilities and an awesome range of fitness classes.
✉ 1001 Brannan St
☎ 552-4653

Taking It to the Streets

Every Friday night about 8pm, weather permitting, hundreds of rollerbladers meet at Justin Herman Plaza for Midnight Rollers, a 12-mile group cruise around downtown and the northern waterfront. On the last Friday of every month, thousands of bicyclists meet at the plaza at 6pm for Critical Mass, a group ride around town that has brought car traffic to a standstill and drivers' tempers to a boil on more than one occasion.

@ www.goldsgym.com
🚌 9 🕐 Mon-Thurs 5am-midnight, Fri 5am-11pm, Sat 7am-9pm, Sun 8am-8pm $ $10 with a member, $15 without a member ♿ yes

Harding Park Golf Course (3, J2)

If you can't get a tee time at the Lincoln Park Golf Course (p. 24, ☎ 221-9911), Harding Park has 18 challenging holes along the Lake Merced shoreline, across from the world-famous Olympic Club course.
✉ 1 Harding Rd
☎ 661-1865 🚌 18, 122 🚊 right on 19th Ave to Winston, right on Lake Merced Dr 🕐 open 6:45am, closing hrs vary from 5pm to 8pm $ $26 weekdays, $31 weekends ♿ yes

Kabuki Springs (4, F3)

Here's the perfect remedy for aches and pains after walking up and down the San Francisco hills. Indulge in the baths at this elegant Japanese spa, get a massage, or treat yourself to a facial (you're worth it). The baths are communal, so check the schedule to confirm which

days are designated for men or women.
✉ 1750 Geary Blvd
☎ 922-6000
@ www.kabuki springs.com 🚌 2, 22, 38 🕐 10am-10pm $ $15-18 (massage and other services extra) ♿ yes

Open Door Yoga (6, F1)

A neighborhood studio offering a full slate of classes all day long, at every level and in every style, including hatha, iyengar, astanga and Pilates.
✉ 1500 Castro St
☎ 824-5657 🚌 24, 48 🕐 Mon-Thurs 7am-9pm, Fri 7am-7:30pm, Sat 9:30am-6pm, Sun 9:30am-8pm
$ $14/class (second class free)

Skates on Haight (2, D9)

These nice people are devoted to skating. They'll teach you how to in-line skate for free every Sunday morning at 9am, in nearby Golden Gate Park between 6th Ave and JFK Dr. They also sponsor a roller disco every Tuesday from 8pm to midnight at Cell Space (1850 Bryant St).
✉ 1818 Haight St
☎ 752-8375 🚌 6, 7, 33, 66, 71 🕐 Mon-Fri 11am-7pm, Sat & Sun 10am-6pm $ $6/hr, $24/day

Sports Hotlines

San Francisco Bicycle Coalition
☎ 431-2453, @ www.sfbike.org

San Francisco Road Runners Club
☎ 273-5731, @ www.sfrrc.org

San Francisco Front Runners
☎ 978-2429, @ www.sffrontrunners.com

San Francisco Board Sailing Association
@ www.sfba.org

Anthony Pidgeon

High winds keep windsurfers and sailors fit all year.

out & about

WALKING TOURS
Union Square to Washington Square

From the Powell St station, walk up Market St toward the Ferry Bldg to 4th St. Cross 4th and turn right, past the Marriott ❶ and into the Metreon ❷, on the other side of Mission St. Go through the lobby of the Metreon into the Yerba Buena Gardens ❸; cut across the gardens and between the buildings to 3rd St. Cross 3rd St and stop at the SF Museum of Modern Art (SFMOMA) ❹. Continue up 3rd to Market St, cross the street and bear left onto Geary St one block before turning right onto Grant Ave. Continue up the sunny

SIGHTS & HIGHLIGHTS

Yerba Buena Gardens (p. 31)
SFMOMA (p. 36)
Old St Mary's Cathedral (p. 39)
Washington Square (p. 41)

Waverly Place

side of Grant past the downtown shops through the Chinatown Gates ❺ at Bush St. Continue past Old St Mary's Cathedral ❻ to Clay St. Turn left and then right on Waverly Place and follow it past the Tien Hau Temple ❼ to Washington St. Turn left on Washington to Stockton St and turn right on Stockton, walking past the markets on the west side of the street and across Broadway into North Beach. Follow Stockton to Columbus Ave, turn left onto Columbus Ave (toward Fisherman's Wharf) and go one block to Washington Square ❽. Cross the square to the church of SS Peter and Paul, on the north side of the street, and then double back to the south side of the square to catch a bus for points north or west.

distance 2 miles (4km) **duration** 2hrs
▶ **start** Ⓜ Powell St station
● **end** Union & Columbus bus stop

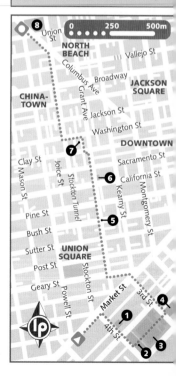

Tales of the City

This walk goes up and down several of the steepest hills in the city. Wear good shoes and take your time. From Union and Hyde Sts, walk east on Union to Leavenworth, turn right and head south one block to Green St, then turn left. The remodeled firehouse on the north side ❶ was the home of Louise Davies, underwriter of the Davies Symphony Hall in the Civic Center. Across the street ❷ is one of two remaining octagon houses in the city (the other is open to the public; see p. 33). At the end of the block, turn left and go downhill a half-block, then turn right into Macondray Lane ❸, inspiration for Barbary Lane in Armistead Maupin's *Tales of the City*. Walk through the lane and down the wooden stairs to Taylor St and turn left to Union St. Turn right and continue down Union past Washington Square ❹ (where Maupin's Mrs Madrigal met Edgar Halcyon), go up the hill to Montgomery St and Speedy's Grocery ❺ (where the father of DeeDee Halcyon Day's twins worked). Turn left and go one block to Filbert St, where DeeDee and Beauchamp lived in the art deco building on the southeast corner ❻ (the building was also featured in the Bogart-Bacall flick *Dark Passage*). Take the Filbert St steps down the hill to Levi Plaza and Park ❼ and the Muni F train home, or alternatively, follow the steps uphill to Coit Tower ❽ and take the 39 bus to Washington Square.

SIGHTS & HIGHLIGHTS

Washington Square (p. 41)
Levi Plaza and Park (p. 40)

Anthony Pidgeon

Coit Tower on Telegraph Hill

---

distance 1 mile (2km) **duration** 2hrs
▶ **start** Union & Hyde Sts
● **end** Filbert St & the Embarcadero

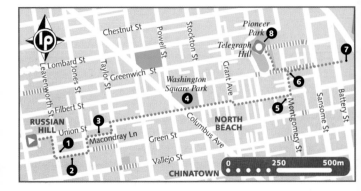

The Castro to the Mission

From the Muni Castro St station, walk down the east side of Castro, past the Castro Theatre **1** to 18th St. Turn left and walk down 18th past Mission High School to Dolores Park **2** and Dolores St. Turn left on Dolores, go two blocks to the Mission Dolores **3**, then turn right on 16th St and follow 16th to Valencia St. Turn right on Valencia and walk down the west side. You'll see the Women's Building **4** from the corner of 18th St, and you'll pass Paxton Gate (p. 42) **5**, a string of book-stores and the eclectic Botanica

SIGHTS & HIGHLIGHTS

Castro Theatre (p. 90)
Women's Building (p. 37)
Mission Dolores (p. 26)

The mural-strewn Women's Building

Anthony Pidgeon

distance 2 miles (4km) **duration** 3hrs
▶ **start** Ⓜ Castro St Muni station
⦿ **end** Ⓜ 24th St BART

Yoruba store on the corner of 21st St **6**. Turn left on 22nd St and walk down the north side of the street past Boogaloo's restaurant **7** and the Mission Market **8**. Turn right on Mission St and walk down the east side of the street, past the shops and markets, to 25th St and La Taqueria **9**. Cross the street and head back toward the 24th St BART station.

Hip Haight

From the Church St Muni station, walk north on Church to Hermann and turn left a half-block to Fillmore St. Turn right on Fillmore, walk up the east side of the street past Sunhee Moon ❶ and the Movida Lounge ❷ (stop for a drink) to Haight St. Turn left on Haight and walk along the south side of the street past Rosamunde Grill ❸ and the Urban School (an alternative school established in the 1960s) ❹, across Divisadero St to Buena Vista Park ❺. At Lyon St, turn right and walk to Janis Joplin's former residence at #112 ❻. Walk back to Haight and continue west to Ashbury St. Turn left and walk to #710, the former Grateful Dead House ❼. Return to Haight on the south side and walk to the Red Victorian B&B ❽, the Red Vic Movie House ❾ and Amoeba Records ❿ until you reach Stanyan St and Golden Gate Park.

SIGHTS & HIGHLIGHTS

Sunhee Moon (p. 58)
Rosamunde Grill (p. 76)
Buena Vista Park (p. 40)
Red Vic Movie House (p. 91)
Golden Gate Park (p. 22)

Anthony Pidgeon

Relive the '60s at Haight and Ashbury.

---

distance 1.6 miles (2km) **duration** 2hrs
▶ **start** Ⓜ Church St Muni station
● **end** Haight & Stanyan bus stop

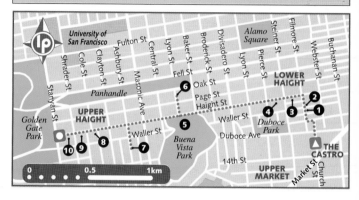

EXCURSIONS
Berkeley
(1, B3)

Before there was a Free Speech Movement, there was a Berkeley. Since the turn of the last century, the original branch of the **University of California** and the town that grew up around it have been centers for free-thinking intellectual life. From the days when Isadora Duncan and her family danced at the Temple of the Winds in the Berkeley Hills, to the 1930s when pacifists roamed the campus, to the 1960s when antiwar protestors took to the streets, 'Berkeley' has been a synonym for 'left-wing' in American life.

INFORMATION

40 miles (64km) east of San Francisco

Ⓜ Downtown Berkeley BART

🚌 AC Transit F bus from Transbay Terminal

🚗 I-80 across Bay Bridge to University Ave exit; east on University to Shattuck Ave and Oxford St

☎ 800-847-4823

ⓔ www.berkeleycvb.com

ⓘ 2015 Center St (Mon-Fri 9am-5pm)

✗ Cafe at Chez Panisse (p. 70)

Berkeley is alive and well today, from the student hangouts along Telegraph Ave south of campus to the **Gourmet Ghetto** north of campus, home of Peet's Coffee (the people who showed the Starbucks people how it's done) and Chez Panisse (home base of Alice Waters, who taught the US about food).

There's much more to see than used-book stores and political posters. The Berkeley campus, home to what is generally considered the best university in the world, is filled with great buildings like the Campanile, copied from the Campanile of Venice, great spaces like the Botanical Gardens and great institutions like the **Berkeley Art Museum and Pacific Film Archive** (p. 34). The hills around the campus have an extraordinary collection of early-20th-century houses by Bay Area architects Bernard Maybeck and Julia Morgan and some of the best views in the entire Bay Area.

The Sather Gate, on the grounds of the University of California, Berkeley

Lee Foster

Monterey Peninsula (1, E3)

The Monterey Peninsula is almost a scale model of the San Francisco Peninsula to the north. There's the historic heart of Monterey, capital of California under the Spanish and the Mexicans, overlooking its own good-size bay. There's a little Fisherman's Wharf and a little military post (now housing a world-famous language school, closed to visitors). There's the village of **Carmel** on the backside, as picture-postcard pretty as Sausalito or Tiburon. Beyond Carmel, there are the Santa Lucia Mountains and **Big Sur**, 90 miles of coastline where the mountains fall into the sea.

It's home to natural wonders like the marine life at **Point Lobos State Reserve** and the monarch butterflies that winter in Pacific Grove. It's home, too, to less-natural wonders like the **Monterey Bay Aquarium** (886 Cannery Row; ☎ 831-648-4888; 10am-6pm Labor Day-Memorial Day, 9:30am-6:30pm Memorial Day-Labor Day; $18/8-15) and the **Pebble Beach Golf Course**. The aquarium is the biggest attraction in town. It's designed to hold a tank large enough to replicate a slice of life in the kelp forests of Monterey Bay, one of the first of its kind when it opened in 1984.

The drive down Hwy 1 from San Francisco affords its own little slice of California coastline scenery. The drive back up US 101 affords a short view of John Steinbeck's central California farm country and a long view of the sprawl of houses and malls that make up most of Silicon Valley.

INFORMATION

250 miles (402km) south of San Francisco

🚗 I-80 south to I-280 to Hwy 1; follow Hwy 1 through Pacifica and Santa Cruz to Monterey and Carmel. Returning, take Hwy 1 north to Hwy 17 in Santa Cruz, take Hwy 17 north to I-280 in San Jose, I-280 north to San Francisco

☎ 888-221-1010

ⓔ www.montereyinfo.org

ⓘ 380 Alvarado St (Mon-Fri 10am-5pm, Sat & Sun 10am-4pm)

✗ Old Monterey Cafe (489 Alvarado St, ☎ 831-646-1021)

Lee Foster

Jellyfish exhibit at Monterey Bay Aquarium

Mt Tamalpais (1, B2)

Like San Francisco, Mt Tamalpais is so lovely you love her on sight. She looms over Marin County north of town like a mountain should, only 2500ft high but carrying herself like a much bigger peak.

Mt Tam is the centerpiece of a set of beautiful state and national parks running from the edges of the suburban towns on the east side of the county all the way to the ocean, from the Golden Gate north to Tomales Bay. Best known of these parks is Muir Woods, a stand of virgin redwoods tucked into a valley of Mt Tam's south slope.

INFORMATION

60 miles (97km) north of San Francisco

🚌 US 101 north across the Golden Gate Bridge to Hwy 1 exit (Stinson Beach); follow signs to the mountain from Hwy 1

☎ 388-2070

ℯ www.cal-parks.ca.gov

ⓘ 801 Panoramic Hwy, Mill Valley (8am-8pm in summer, 10am-6pm other seasons)

◷ standard time 7am-6pm, daylight-saving 7am-sunset

✕ Mountain Home Inn (810 Panoramic Hwy, Mill Valley; ☎ 381-9000)

Up on the mountain, 50 miles of hiking and biking trails connect with 200 more miles of Marin County trails. (The mountain bike was invented here, by local kids who needed special equipment for the steep grades and rough roads.) There are picnic grounds and campgrounds and the Mountain Theater, a 3700-seat amphitheater that has hosted the Mountain Play every spring since 1913.

All of this comes with those amazing Bay Area views. From the woods on the flank of the mountain, hikers emerge into meadows with views of the Golden Gate Bridge and the ocean. From the East Peak summit, you can see the whole Bay Area, from the hills beyond San Jose in the south to Mt St Helena and the valleys of the wine country in the north.

The reward for a long hike

Napa Valley   (1, A2)

An hour and a half north of the city, a long, narrow valley combines the wild beauty of the American West with the settled beauty of France or Italy.

It takes shape as you near the city of Napa, toward its south end. In the foreground, vineyards and buildings appear on the flat valley floor. In the background, half-mile-high ridges on either side are covered with dusty pines and brush. In the distance is the cinder cone of Mt St Helena, the little volcano (long extinct) that dumped the rich volcanic ash that makes these vineyards thrive.

In the middle of all this scenery, there's an incomparable world of wine and food. The wine did come first, going toe to toe with European vintages in the 1970s, but the food followed quickly. Today, there are great restaurants in every town from Napa to Calistoga, good bakeries and coffee shops and even a couple of choice dives.

INFORMATION

140 miles (225km) north of San Francisco

🚗 I-80 east across the Bay Bridge, past Carquinez Bridge to Hwy 29 exit; take Hwy 29 north to St Helena and beyond

☎ 707-226-7459

e www.napavalley.com

ⓘ 1310 Napa Town Center, Napa (9am-5pm, closed Easter, Thanksgiving, Christmas & New Year's Day)

✕ Mustard's Grill (7399 St Helena Hwy/Hwy 29, Yountville; ☎ 707-944-2424)

It's beautiful any time of year, from rainy days in the winter, when the brown vine stumps shine against the grass and mustard in the fields, to hot summer days, when the green vineyards glisten against the dull brown hills.

More than 200 wineries lie just an hour and a half away in Napa Valley.

ORGANIZED TOURS

Several companies run bus tours of the main sights, but you can make up your own tour by riding the Muni 22, 38 or F lines. (Avoid the 22 after school and after dark.) You can also organize your own informal boat tour around the bay by taking one of the commuter ferries from the Ferry Building (5, F8) to Sausalito, Larkspur, Oakland or Vallejo. Self-guided bike tours are outlined on the map you get when you rent a bike at Blazing Saddles (p. 44), or you can join Critical Mass on the last Friday of the month (p. 45). Walking tours are available almost everywhere anytime, most run by cultural institutions or individuals.

Blue & Gold Fleet
(5, A3) This company offers a one-hour tour that loops under the Golden Gate Bridge and around Alcatraz, as well as tours of Angel Island, ferries to Vallejo, Marin County and Pacific Bell Park, and bus tours of city locations.
✉ **Pier 39 ☎ 773-1188** ⏲ **bay cruises 10am-4pm ⑤ bay cruises $18/10-14 (Web specials at** e **www.blueand goldfleet.com)**

Cruisin' the Castro
(6, C1) Trevor Hailey's walking tour of the Castro covers the landmarks and the history of San Francisco's gay community, from the Twin Peaks Bar to Harvey Milk's camera shop.
✉ **meet at Harvey Milk Plaza, Castro & Market Sts ☎ 550-8110** ⏲ **Tues-Sat 10am-2pm ⑤ $40 (lunch included)**

Gray Line
(5, H7) The biggest tour company in town offers six different bus tours departing from downtown hotels, including tours on motorized cable cars (approximating some of the pleasures of riding the cable cars without standing in line). Dress warmly.
✉ **most tours depart Transbay Terminal ☎ 558-7300** ⏲ **daily from 9am ⑤ basic tours $15-37 (bay cruises, walks, helicopter tours extra)**

Heritage Tours (4, D4)
The Foundation for San Francisco's Architectural Heritage runs two-hour tours of the mansions and simpler houses of Pacific Heights every Sunday afternoon.
✉ **meet at Haas-Lilienthal House, 2007 Franklin St ☎ 441-3004** ⏲ **Sunday 12:30pm ⑤ $5/3**

Neighborhood Walks
Walking tours of neighborhoods, including the Mission, North Beach, Pacific Heights and Japantown, are organized under the auspices of the San Francisco Public Library and staffed by volunteers. Call in advance for details.
☎ **557-4266** ⏲ **May-Oct, schedules vary ⑤ free**

Red & White Fleet
(5, A2) The Red & White Fleet boats do a one-hour loop under the Golden Gate Bridge and around Alcatraz from their dock at Fisherman's Wharf.
✉ **Pier 43½ ☎ 673-2900** ⏲ **mid-Sept–March 10am-4:15pm, April–mid-Sept 10am-6:15pm ⑤ $18/10-14**

San Francisco Seaplane Tours (5, A3)
Try a 30-minute flight in an old-fashioned de Havilland seaplane that takes you soaring over the city, the bridges, Sausalito, Tiburon and the Marin County parks.
✉ **Pier 39 ☎ 332-4843** ⏲ **flights daily, call ahead for schedule ⑤ $129/99**

Victorian Home Walks
(5, J4) A sampler of Victoriana includes row houses, mansions and the commercial strip of Union St in Cow Hollow. See the inside of a Victorian and outsides of other homes not seen on the bus tours.
✉ **meet at Westin St Francis Hotel, 335 Powell St, for Muni ride to Pacific Heights ☎ 252-9485** ⏲ **11am (except Christmas & New Year's Day) ⑤ $20**

Sightseeing by cable car

shopping

Shopping is San Francisco's secret pleasure. Too-conspicuous consumption is antithetical to that San Francisco anti-style. However, there's an enormous amount of money around, so there are an enormous number of stores to spend that money in, from branches of all the great logos and names to one-offs that thrive in these well-heeled, vaguely bohemian surroundings. You'll find almost anything here that you'd find in London or Los Angeles, all within a few square blocks downtown or on one of a few nearby neighborhood shopping streets.

Shopping Districts

Union Square is the heart of the action – New York's 34th St, 57th St and Madison Ave all rolled into one. An elegance lingers from the days ladies wore white gloves when they came downtown, alongside the contemporary slouch style of Niketown. The mix of great department stores, international luxury emporia, small local boutiques, hotels and theaters keeps the streets humming.

Beyond Van Ness Ave, the smart set from Pacific Heights and Presidio Heights wander the shops lining **Fillmore St**, **Sacramento St** and **Union St**. Across town, **Valencia St** and **Haight St** present an only-in-San Francisco mixture of used clothes, books and records, and hip boutiques with the occasional auto-body repair shop thrown in for good measure.

Anthony Pidgeon

Vintage clothes, hipster shoes, pipes and music for sale on Haight St

DEPARTMENT STORES & SHOPPING CENTERS

Embarcadero Center
(5, F6) Three floors of courtyards, walkways and shops form the base of this complex of office buildings running from the Embarcadero east to Battery St. You'll find mostly chain stores plus a sensational movie theater, some good restaurants, a post office and other amenities.
✉ **bounded by Sacramento St, the Embarcadero, Clay St & Battery St** ☎ 772-0734 Ⓜ **Embarcadero, California cable car** 🚌 1, 2, 41 🕐 Mon-Fri 10am-7pm, Sat 10am-6pm, Sun noon-5pm

Macy's (5, J4)
This is the West Coast flagship of the Macy's chain, the laboratory where the Macy's people play with what goes in a department store. It has good clothing departments for men, women and children, and great specialty departments from kitchenware in the basement to linens up above.
✉ **170 O'Farrell St** ☎ 397-3333 Ⓜ **Powell, Powell-Hyde & Powell-Mason cable cars** 🚌 2, 30, 38 🕐 Mon-Wed 10am-

8pm, Thurs-Sat 10am-9pm, Sun 11am-7pm

Neiman-Marcus (5, J4)
When you're looking for the extraordinary and you're willing to pay for it, this is the place. Bring your checkbook or an American Express card, because it's one of the few places in the civilized world that does not take Visa or MasterCard.
✉ **150 Stockton St** ☎ 362-3900 Ⓜ **Powell, Powell-Hyde & Powell-Mason cable cars** 🚌 2, 30, 38 🕐 10am-7pm (Thurs to 8pm)

Nordstrom (5, K4)
A great selection of men's and women's shoes and a solid if unexciting collection of good-quality clothes and accessories are all presented to you by an accommodating sales staff.
✉ **865 Market St** ☎ 243-8500 Ⓜ **Powell, Powell-Hyde & Powell-Mason cable cars** 🚌 5, 6, 7, 66, 71 🕐 Mon-Sat 9:30am-9pm, Sun 10am-7pm

Saks Fifth Avenue
(5, J4) The usual collection of high-end women's clothes and cosmetics is nicely assembled in a

The Embarcadero

smallish location on the sunny side of Union Square. The Men's Store down the street at 220 Post St is closer to the cutting edge, with casual clothes to match traditional strengths in business wear.
✉ **384 Post St** ☎ 986-4300 Ⓜ **Powell, Powell-Hyde & Powell-Mason cable cars** 🚌 2, 30, 38 🕐 Mon-Sat 10am-7pm (Thurs to 8pm), Sun 11am-6pm

San Francisco Shopping Centre
(5, K4) This shopping mall in the middle of town turns conventional mall planning on its head. The boutiques (mainly branches of the chains you see in suburban malls) are on the first three floors, and the anchor – Nordstrom – is on the top. Otherwise, it's best known for its curving escalators.
✉ **865 Market St** ☎ 495-5656 Ⓜ **Powell, Powell-Hyde & Powell-Mason cable cars** 🚌 5, 6, 7, 66, 71 🕐 Mon-Sat 9:30am-8pm, Sun 11am-6pm

Outlet Malls
The garlic capital of Gilroy, south of San Jose, is also the outlet capital of the Bay Area. The **Premium Outlets of Gilroy** (681 Leavesley Rd at US 101, ☎ 408-842-3729) has 150 stores, including Big Dog, Kenneth Cole and Lenox China. North of San Francisco, the **Petaluma Village Outlet Mall** (2200 Petaluma Blvd North at US 101, ☎ 707-778-9300) is a little smaller and more upscale (if that's not an oxymoron for an outlet mall).

MARKETS

If Northern California is in fact the France of the US, it's no surprise that San Francisco has a wealth of food markets and farmer's markets.

Berkeley Farmer's Market (7, C4 & A4)

The Berkeley Ecology Center has sponsored this market for the past 10 years. Over half the produce is certified organic. There's also fresh bread, olive oils, cheeses and prepared foods to tempt the hungry.

✉ **Derby St & Martin Luther King Jr Dr (Tues), Center St & Martin Luther King Jr Dr (Sat), Berkeley** ☎ **510-548-3333** Ⓜ **Downtown Berkeley BART** 🚌 **AC Transit F bus from Transbay Terminal** ⓧ **Tues 2pm-7pm, Sat 10am-3pm**

Ferry Plaza Farmer's Market (5, E6)

The Ferry Plaza Farmers' Market will return to its space in front of the Ferry Building in late 2003. In the meantime, it brings the bounty of California's farms and kitchens to Justin Herman Plaza (5, F7) on Tuesday and to Levi Plaza on Saturday.

✉ **Embarcadero at Green St** ☎ **535-5650** Ⓜ **Embarcadero, Muni F line** ⓧ **Tues 10:30am-2:30pm, Sat 8am-1:30pm**

Market Hall (7, D6)

The best food market in the Bay Area is in the Rockridge section of Oakland, south of Berkeley, steps from the Rockridge BART station. Eight sensational shops sell everything from produce and pasta to meat and fish. It's mayhem on Saturday, a delight the rest of the time.

✉ **5655 College Ave, Oakland** ☎ **510-655-7748** Ⓜ **Rockridge BART** ⓧ **Mon-Fri 10am-8pm, Sat & Sun 10am-7pm**

San Francisco Flower Mart (5, M6)

More than 80 vendors sell fresh flowers and anything else floral. All welcome retail customers (it's wholesale only earlier in the day), and many take credit cards. Poke around and have breakfast or coffee at the Flower Mart Café, but note that it's busy on Saturday morning and holidays.

✉ **640 Brannan St** ☎ **781-8410** 🚌 **10, 47** ⓧ **Mon-Sat 10am-3pm**

United Nations Plaza Farmer's Market (5, L3)

This is the working-guy's farmer's market, where Southeast Asian immigrants from the Tenderloin shop along with government workers and simple citizens who don't need the glamour of the Ferry Plaza markets. You won't find the fancy stuff, but you'll still find the fresh.

✉ **UN Plaza, Market & 7th Sts** ☎ **558-9455** Ⓜ **Civic Center** 🚌 **5, 6, 7, 66, 71** ⓧ **Wed & Sun 7am-5pm**

The Ferry Plaza hosts a farmer's market.

CLOTHING

Amid the options, a few themes repeat: San Franciscans are not slaves to fashion, though they appreciate expressions of personal style. Clothing styles lean to the Italian and the Asian when not indigenously American (the blue jean was invented here, after all). San Franciscans are willing to spend money for something that fits or wears well, but less willing to spend for something that's the color or style of the moment.

BILLYBLUE (5, J5)

Come here for menswear from Milan (and elsewhere in Italy) and from American clothiers who speak, or at least appreciate, Italian. Find one-off designs that deliver European style with American comfort.

✉ **54 Geary St**
☎ **781-2111**
Ⓜ **Montgomery or Powell** 🚌 2, 3, 4, 15, 30, 38 🕐 **Mon-Sat 10am-6pm**

Bulo (4, G4)

You'll find a fine selection of trendy shoes, from Adidas and Pumas in the hottest colors and styles to the big names like Prada. Now also uptown, with a branch at 3044 Fillmore St (4, C3; ☎ 614-9959) in the heart of Cow Hollow.

✉ **418 & 453 Hayes St**
☎ **225-4935** 🚌 21
🕐 **Mon-Sat 11am-6:30pm, Sun noon-6pm**

HRM Boutique

(6, D4) There's nothing casual about the casual clothes for men and women here. Designed and sewn in-house, they have everything you like about Banana Republic (comfort, panache) without the worry that every third person on the street will be wearing your outfit.

✉ **924 Valencia St**
☎ **642-0841** 🚌 14, 26, 49 🕐 **noon-7pm**

MAC (5, H5)

Modern Appealing Clothing for men and women is the theme, at the men's store in a lane near Union Square and at the women's store on upper Grant Ave in North Beach (1543 Grant Ave; 5, D4; ☎ 837-1604). You'll get designers like Paul Smith and Kenzo, and lesser names affording similar style and comfort.

✉ **5 Claude Ln**
☎ **837-0615**
Ⓜ **Montgomery or**

Powell 🚌 2, 3, 4, 15, 30 🕐 Mon-Sat 11am-6pm, Sun noon-5pm

Rolo (5, J4)

A range of trendy clothes for men and women: The downtown and Castro St stores (450 Castro St; 6, C1; ☎ 626-7171) focus on everyday items like jeans and shoes. The Market St location (2351 Market St; 6, C1; ☎ 431-4545) runs upmarket, with designers like Helmut Lang and Comme des Garçons.

✉ **21 Stockton St**
☎ **989-7656** Ⓜ **Powell** 🚌 5, 6, 7, 30, 66, 71 🕐 **11am-7pm (Castro & Market St to 8pm Mon-Sat)**

Shoe Biz (2, C10)

These are seriously trendy shoes for men and women. Find slightly less trendy stuff, like the Pumas of the moment, at the sister store down the block (1553 Haight St, ☎ 861-3933).

✉ **1446 Haight St**
☎ **864-0990** 🚌 6, 7, 33, 43, 66, 71 🕐 **Mon-Sat 11am-7pm, Sun noon-6pm**

Sunhee Moon (6, A2)

Clean, classic California sportswear for women with an edge of Asian styling are all designed by Ms Moon for her boutique in the Lower Haight.

✉ **142 Fillmore St**

Vintage Vestments

There may be more and better used-clothing stores here than in any other city in the country. At the top of the food chain, you'll find designer clothes on consignment in the boutiques along outer Sacramento St. In between, try the string of thrift shops run by fancy charities along Fillmore St in Pacific Heights. Bottom feeders can prowl the used-clothing shops that dot Valencia St and Haight St.

☎ 355-1800 Ⓜ Muni
N line 🚃 6, 7, 22, 66,
71 ⏰ Mon-Fri noon-
6pm, Sat & Sun noon-
5pm

Villains (2, D9)
The clothes here are for
teens and 20-somethings
with a taste for hip-hop
styles. Slightly more
upscale gear from Diesel
and other designers can be
found at the Villains Vault
across the street (1653
Haight St, ☎ 864-7727).
✉ **1672 Haight St**
☎ **626-5939** 🚃 6, 7,
33, 43, 66, 71
⏰ **11am-7pm**

Wilkes Bashford
(5, H4) A San Francisco
institution for more than
30 years, this store has five
floors of the finest fashions

for men and women.
Surrender yourself and your
credit cards to a salesper-
son and see where the
best Italian, French and
American designers can
take you.
✉ **375 Sutter St**
☎ **986-4380** Ⓜ **Powell**
🚃 **2, 3, 4, 30** ⏰ **Mon-
Sat 10am-6pm (Thurs
to 8pm)**

Zoe (3, D5)
This local boutique has
high-fashion clothes and
shoes from French and
American designers and
offers easy, sexy alternatives to those architectural
styles from Milan or Tokyo.
Vive la différence.
✉ **3571 Sacramento St**
☎ **929-0441** 🚃 1
⏰ **Mon-Sat 11am-7pm,
Sun noon-5pm**

Chain Gang
If you're looking for
branches of the big
American chains like
**Gap, Abercrombie,
The Limited, Ann
Taylor** or **Foot Locker**,
you'll find them in **Em-
barcadero Center**, the
**San Francisco Shop-
ping Centre** and in
free-standing locations
around Union Square.

Chains galore downtown

ANTIQUES & FURNITURE

Unlike some other places in the country, the best antique and furniture
stores here are open to the public, which means you can wander through
showrooms formerly limited to decorators and clients. The showrooms are
conveniently clustered in Jackson Square (Jackson St between Chinatown
and the water) and at the foot of Potrero Hill along Henry Adams St.

Butterfield's (5, P4)
The biggest auction
house in the West (now a
division of eBay) auctions
fine art and furniture on a
regular schedule and also
runs estate sales of lower-
ticket items. Call ahead or
check online at the web-
site, 🅴 www.butter
fields.com, to see what's
coming on the auction
block.
✉ **220 San Bruno Ave**
☎ **861-7500** 🚃 9, 22
⏰ **Mon-Fri 8:30am-
5pm, open Sat & Sun
for previews in
advance of auctions;
call ahead**

Big Pagoda (4, E3)
Although some of the
tables and chests on the
floor are antiques from
China, the most interesting
pieces in the store are
tables and cabinets made
in China to Big Pagoda
specifications using traditional materials and
designs.
✉ **1903 Fillmore St**
☎ **563-8727** 🚃 2, 3,
4, 22 ⏰ **Tues-Sat
11am-7pm, Sun
noon-6pm**

Den (6, D4)
Mid-20th-century furniture
meets modern furniture

with a mid-century, Rae-
and-Charles-Eames atti-
tude. Like its neighbors
along Valencia St, it's
about high style at mid-
dling prices.
✉ **849 Valencia St**
☎ **282-6649** 🚃 14, 26
⏰ **Wed-Sat noon-7pm,
Sun noon-6pm**

**Evelyn's Antique
Chinese Furniture**
(4, H5) The Chinese furniture and furnishings in the
front rooms here can keep
you busy for an hour, but
the collection in the back,
some awaiting repair or
refinishing, can keep you

Jackson Square

looking all afternoon.
✉ **381 Hayes St**
☎ **255-1815** Ⓜ **Muni Van Ness** 🚌 **21, 47, 49**
🕐 **Mon-Sat 10:30am-6:30pm**

Genji Antiques (4, F4)
A big barn of a place in the Miyako Wing of the Japan Center, filled with chests and cabinets and odd bits like doors and bamboo fencing. For those in the market for soft goods, there are kimonos, sashes and textiles.
✉ **22 Peace Plaza**
☎ **931-1616** 🚌 **2, 3, 4, 22, 38** 🕐 **Mon-Sat 10am-6pm, Sun 11am-6pm**

Gump's (5, H5)
Since 1861, San Franciscans have come to Gump's for luxury goods from Europe and Asia like sparkling china and crystal, sensual silk and jade. The store has passed from the Gump family into corporate hands, but it retains their East-West point of view.
✉ **135 Post St** ☎ **982-1616** Ⓜ **Montgomery** 🚌 **2, 3, 4, 15, 30**
🕐 **Mon-Sat 10am-6pm**

Limn Furniture (5, M7)
If you have a weakness for modern furniture, particularly modern furniture from Italy in a sleek showroom, leave your checkbook at home before you wander through Limn Furniture. An enormous selection of the best stuff in the best taste.
✉ **290 Townsend St**
☎ **543-5466** Ⓜ **Muni F line** 🚌 **10, 30, 45, 47**
🕐 **Mon-Fri 9:30am-6pm, Sat & Sun 11am-6pm**

Peter Pap Oriental Rugs (5, F5)
Peter Pap and his crew are passionate about carpets and textiles, so don't let the splendor of the goods on the floor scare you away. See a lot and maybe even learn a little in the process.
✉ **470 Jackson St**
☎ **956-3300** 🚌 **10, 15, 41** 🕐 **Mon-Sat 10am-5pm**

Zonal (4, E3)
San Franciscans are as quick to display their bohemian credentials as the typical resident of Soho. The four Zonal stores around town are places where one can find the industrial-toned furniture and furnishings (much of it designed here) to make a loft a home.
✉ **1942 Fillmore St**
☎ **359-9111** 🚌 **2, 3, 4, 22** 🕐 **Tues-Sat 11am-6pm, Sun noon-5pm**

Worship at the Big Pagoda, on swank Fillmore St

ARTS & CRAFTS

Cradle of the Sun
(6, E2) This is one of the places Victorian-home owners go for stained-glass windows or furnishings to help set their houses right. A great place for the adult eye. A bad place for children.
✉ 3948 24th St ☎ 821-7667 Ⓜ Muni J line 🚌 48 🕘 Tues-Sat 10am-6pm, Sun 1pm-4pm

Flax Art (4, H5)
Called a 'candy store for the creative,' this family-owned emporium stocks everything in the way of art supplies. One could spend hours dawdling over the selection of papers alone but for the siren call of the pens in their counters nearby.
✉ 1699 Market St ☎ 552-2355 Ⓜ Muni Van Ness 🚌 6, 7, 66, 71 🕘 Mon-Sat 9:30am-6pm (Thurs to 7pm)

Folk Art International Gallery
(5, J4) Frank Lloyd Wright designed this space, tucked into the most charming Union Square lane. Inside, it's filled with folk art in every size, shape and form.
✉ 140 Maiden Ln ☎ 392-9999 Ⓜ Powell 🚌 2, 3, 4, 30, 38 🕘 Mon-Sat 10am-6pm

Global Exchange
(6, F2) Handicrafts from all over the developing world are imported by the Global Exchange people as part of their global effort to promote fair trade.
✉ 4018 24th St ☎ 648-8068 Ⓜ Muni J line 🚌 24, 48 🕘 11am-7pm (Sat from 10am)

Japonesque Gallery
(5, F5) This collection of Japanese art and artifacts is so elegant you could mistake it for a museum. Some old, some new, all highly refined in sensibility.
✉ 824 Montgomery St ☎ 563-2970 🚌 10, 15, 41 🕘 Wed-Sun 11am-7pm

Indoarts (3, D5)
Carvings, puppets, jewelry, furniture and textiles from Bali and Java fill this tiny shop in Presidio Heights, alongside a selection of other arts & crafts from other countries and cultures. The common denominators are beauty and delight.
✉ 3424 Sacramento St ☎ 922-5131 🚌 1, 43 🕘 Tues-Sat 10am-6pm

Surprise Party (4, E3)
A cornucopia of beads and shells and things made with beads and shells, including a dazzling array of necklaces made of turquoise and other big semiprecious stones. The tiny space is jammed with merchandise, so watch your elbows.
✉ 1900A Fillmore St ☎ 771-8550 🚌 2, 3, 4, 22 🕘 Tues-Sun noon-6pm

Anthony Pidgeon

Folk Art International, designed by Frank Lloyd Wright

FOOD & DRINK

Bi-Rite Market (6, C3)
This neighborhood market that crams everything a serious cook (or eater) could desire in a smallish space looks like it hasn't changed since it opened in 1940. Come for a wine and cheese selection to match any gourmet shop, and in-store music that would satisfy the lads from *High Fidelity*.
✉ **3639 18th St**
☎ **241-9773 Ⓜ Muni J line 🚌 33** ◷ **Mon-Fri 10am-9pm, Sat 9am-8pm, Sun 9am-7pm**

Bryan's (3, D5)
Bryan's has the best meat, fish and poultry available retail in this food-obsessed town. Were that not enough, the selection of prepared foods, fresh fruits and vegetables means one-stop shopping (two stops if you want wine).
✉ **3473 California St**
☎ **752-3430 🚌 1** ◷ **Mon-Fri 8am-7pm, Sat 8am-6pm**

Ghirardelli Soda Fountain & Chocolate Shop (4, A5)
Stock up on chocolaty snacks and gifts here at the flagship store in Ghirardelli Square.
✉ **900 North Point St**
☎ **474-3938** ◷ **Sun-Thurs 9am-11pm, Fri & Sat 9am-midnight**
🚌 **19, 30, 42**

Joseph Schmidt Confections (6, C2)
Joseph Schmidt was trained as a baker in Europe, but when he opened his bakery and chocolate shop in 1983, the chocolates flew out the door and he forgot about pastries. Come in and peruse the truffles, chocolate logs and chocolate tree sculptures.
✉ **3489 16th St**
☎ **861-8682 Ⓜ Muni Church or Castro**
🚌 **22** ◷ **Mon-Sat 10am-6:30pm**

Kermit Lynch Wine Merchant (7, A2)
Kermit Lynch, the man who brought reasonably priced European wines to Northern California, is a key figure in the Berkeley food pantheon. The original store, next to Alice Waters' Cafe Fanny and the original outlet of the Acme Bakery, is a must-see on any foodie's pilgrimage.
✉ **1605 San Pablo Ave, Berkeley** ☎ **510-524-1524** 🚗 **east on I-80, over Bay Bridge to Gilman exit, east on Gilman to San Pablo, south on San Pablo to corner of Cedar**
◷ **Tues-Sat 11am-6pm**

Molinari Delicatessen (5, E4) The great North Beach Italian delicatessen has been serving up meats, cheeses and pastas to neighbors and sons and daughters from the old neighborhood for generations. It also serves up sandwiches to anyone planning on a picnic in one of the neighborhood parks.
✉ **373 Columbus Ave**
☎ **421-2337** 🚌 **15, 30, 45** ◷ **Mon-Fri 8am-6pm, Sat 7:30am-5:30pm**

Peets Coffee and Tea (5, F1) Peets is a local favorite, but not everyone can handle its strong, dark coffee. Try it for yourself, and decide if you want to buy a pound or two. Other branches are scattered around the Bay Area.
✉ **2139 Polk St**
☎ **474-1871** 🚌 **12, 19** ◷ **Mon-Fri 6:30am-7pm, Sat & Sun 7am-7pm**

PlumpJack Wines (4, C2) An uncommonly good wine shop, Plump-Jack is fancy enough for Pacific Heights matrons and easy enough for the rest of us. There's a wide selection and a staff who don't mind helping you decide.
✉ **3201 Fillmore St**
☎ **346-9870** 🚌 **22** ◷ **Mon-Sat 11am-8pm, Sun 11am-6pm**

Safeway (6, B3)
This supermarket and its mate, the Marina Safeway (15 Marina Blvd, ☎ 563-4946), are some of the best stores in the chain. They're also reputed as two of the hottest pick-up spots in town.
✉ **2020 Market St**
☎ **861-7660 Ⓜ Muni Church** 🚌 **22, 37** ◷ **24-7**

Stella Pastry and Cafe (5, E3)
Even San Franciscans who rarely venture to North Beach make the trek to Stella for the St Honore cake, the Italian pastries and cookies, and old-fashioned espresso to wash it all down. Consider buying a scripantina, a rich sponge

cake with liqueur and cream.

✉ **446 Columbus Ave**
☎ **986-2914**
🚌 **15, 30, 41, 45**
🕐 Oct-May 7:30am-6pm, June-Sept 7:30am-10pm

Whole Foods (4, E4)
This model of bourgeois bohemian shopping has a great delicatessen, good produce and prepared foods – they deliver to all the better zip codes across the country.

✉ **1765 California St**
☎ **674-0500**
Ⓜ **California cable car**
🚌 **47, 49**
🕐 8am-10pm

Bread Lines

San Francisco has been famous for bread since the miners made sourdough during the gold rush. The food revolution of the 1970s brought all kinds of bakers onto the scene, producing everything from baguettes good enough for France to savory whole-wheat walnut loafs. Our favorites are **Boulangerie Bay Bread** (2325 Pine St; 4, E3; ☎ 440-0356), **Noe Valley Bakery** (4073 24th St; 6, F2; ☎ 550-1405) and **Acme Bakery** in Berkeley (1601 San Pablo Ave; 7, A2; ☎ 510-843-2978).

Wine Club (5, M5)
This warehouse near the Hall of Justice looks more like the Fight Club than the Wine Club. Don't be put off by appearances. It's the best bet for wine in the city. Come and educate your palate with wines on offer for tasting (you must be 21), or ask the staff for some help.

✉ **953 Harrison St**
☎ **512-9086** 🚌 **27, 47**
🕐 Mon-Sat 9am-7pm, Sun 11am-6pm

Clam chowder in a sourdough loaf, a Fisherman's Wharf staple

Anthony Pidgeon

BOOKS & MUSIC

A Clean Well Lighted Place for Books (4, G5)
The best general bookstore in the city and one of the best independent bookstores in the country, this place is known for a full calendar of literary events and for a staff that actually know and read books
✉ Opera Plaza, 601 Van Ness Ave ☎ 441-6670 Ⓜ Muni Van Ness 🚌 47, 49 ⏰ Mon-Sat 10am-11pm, Sun 10am-9pm

A Different Light
(6, C1) This is the premiere gay and lesbian bookstore, featuring fiction and nonfiction, travel literature, poetry, cards and photographs since 1979. Check its calendar for literary events of interest to the community.
✉ 489 Castro St ☎ 431-0891 Ⓜ Muni Castro 🚌 24, 33, 35 ⏰ 10am-midnight

Aquarius Records
(6, E4) You've probably never heard any of the groups or recordings on the pick-of-the-week board

out front, but that's why you go to a laid-back place like this for alternative (punk, grunge, experimental, imports) music.
✉ 1055 Valencia St ☎ 647-2272 Ⓜ 24th St BART 🚌 14, 26 ⏰ Mon-Wed 10am-9pm, Thurs-Sun 10am-10pm

City Lights (5, F4)
More than just a bookstore, this is the shop Lawrence Ferlinghetti wrought. It's an alternative press (they still crank out copies of Allen Ginsberg's poem 'Howl') and a platform for writers, poets and activists presenting alternatives to the mainstream. If you can't find it at Borders, try here.
✉ 261 Columbus Ave ☎ 362-8193 🚌 15, 30, 41, 45 ⏰ 10am-midnight

Cody's Books (7, B5)
Cody's is one of those institutions that made Berkeley Berkeley. It publishes poetry, sponsors literary events and even spruces up the streetscape

with its little plaza on Telegraph Ave. Visit Cody's here or at the new branch on Fourth St in west Berkeley (1730 4th St; 7, A1; ☎ 510-559-9500), the Rodeo Drive of the Birkenstock set.
✉ 2454 Telegraph Ave, Berkeley ☎ 510-845-7852 Ⓜ Downtown Berkeley BART 🚌 AC Transit F bus from Transbay Terminal ⏰ 10am-10pm

Discolandia (3, G8)
The great granddaddy of the Latin music scene, reflecting the diversity of the Latino community in the Mission, this store has everything from merengue and salsa to the accordion strains of Tejano. A good selection of books and magazines round out the offerings.
✉ 2964 24th St ☎ 826-9446 🚌 48 ⏰ Mon-Sat 11:30am-6:30pm, Sun noon-4pm

Get Lost (6, A3)
The best travel bookstore in San Francisco, Get Lost has travel guides, travel literature and events

Books about San Francisco
There are lots of books set in San Francisco but surprisingly few books *about* San Francisco. Amy Tan's *Joy Luck Club* tells a great deal about Chinese American women living in the city. Armistead Maupin's *Tales of the City* is the best of the lot, an affectionate look at the small-town connections between all the wildly different people who've come to live here. Dashiell Hammett's *The Maltese Falcon* paints a picture of the city in the 1930s that still comes to mind on dark, foggy nights in Chinatown.

Anthony Pidgeon

Browse the shelves of City Lights with Lawrence Ferlinghetti.

about one or the other. There's a good selection of gear and a sensational selection of maps lining the shelves.

✉ **1825 Market St**
☎ **437-0529** Ⓜ **Muni Van Ness** ◷ **Mon-Fri 10am-7pm, Sat 10am-6pm, Sun 11am-5pm**

Green Apple Books
(2, A7) The largest used-book store in the city has piles and piles of books on every subject imaginable in every condition, along with a good selection of secondhand records and CDs. Come pan for gold amid the shelves.

✉ **506 Clement St**
☎ **387-2272** 🚌 **1, 2, 38, 44** ◷ **Sun-Thurs 10am-10:30pm, Fri & Sat 10am-11:30pm**

Rizzoli Bookstore
(5, J5) A throwback to the days of Charles Dickens or at least F Scott Fitzgerald, this quiet bookstore feels like the library of a posh club. You'll find a very strong selection of art, architecture and design books as well as an espresso bar upstairs.

✉ **117 Post St**
☎ **984-0225**
Ⓜ **Montgomery or Powell** 🚌 **2, 3, 4, 15, 30, 38** ◷ **Mon-Sat 10am-6pm**

Tower Records (5, C2)
Tower Records started in a corner of the Solomon family pharmacy in Sacramento. When Russ Solomon decided it was time to try a big, freestanding record store of his own, he settled here on the

edge of the Wharf. There are Towers around the world these days, but it's still hard to beat the original for selection or prices.

✉ **2525 Jones St**
☎ **885-0500** 🚌 **30, 41** ◷ **Sun-Thurs 10am-11pm, Fri & Sat 10am-midnight**

William K Stout Architectural Books
(5, F5) Books about anything to do with architecture and design line the shelves, from picture books for the coffee table to how-to books on new construction modes. Read up on rammed-earth houses or the Bauhaus.

✉ **804 Montgomery St**
☎ **391-6757** 🚌 **15, 30, 41, 45** ◷ **Mon-Fri 10am-6pm, Sat 10am-5:30pm**

FOR CHILDREN

The best shopping for children in San Francisco is in Laurel Heights (California St between Laurel and Spruce Sts) and Presidio Heights (Sacramento St from Presidio Ave to Spruce St).

Dottie Doolittle
(3, D5) If Bergdorf Goodman had a children's department, this is what it would look like: infant and toddlers' clothes for boys and girls, and classic clothes for girls four to 14, including fancy party dresses and all the requisite accessories.
✉ **3680 Sacramento St**
☎ **563-3244** 🚌 **1, 43**
🕐 **Mon-Sat 9:30am-6pm, Sun noon-5pm**

Esprit Outlet (3, F10)
This is a good place to take a girl or two, aged five to 15 or 20, to get snappy Esprit clothes at snappy outlet-store prices. It's probably a bad place to take three or four girls unless you have training as an elementary school teacher or a sheep dog (too much to see, too many places to scatter).
✉ **499 Illinois St**
☎ **957-2550** 🚌 **15**
🕐 **Mon-Fri 10am-8pm, Sat 10am-7pm, Sun 11am-6pm (closed Easter, Thanksgiving & Christmas)**

FAO Schwarz (5, J4)
Every week is the week before Christmas at FAO Schwarz. Three floors are filled with toys, stuffed animals, Legos and action figures from the latest blockbusters.
✉ **48 Stockton St**
☎ **394-8700** 🚇 **Powell, Powell-Mason & Powell-Hyde cable cars** 🚌 **6, 7, 9, 30**

🕐 **Mon-Sat 11am-7pm, Sun noon-7pm**

Jeffrey's Toys (5, J5)
This is a throwback to another era when toys came from places smaller and homier than the Toys"R"Us on the freeway. Barbies, comics and action figures will make the kids happy.
✉ **7 3rd St** ☎ **243-8697** 🚇 **Montgomery** 🚌 **5, 6, 7, 15, 30**
🕐 **Mon-Fri 9am-8pm, Sat 10am-8pm, Sun 11am-6pm**

Jonathan-Kaye (3, D5)
Furniture and furnishings for children's rooms come in traditional styles, from tiny rocking chairs to bunk beds and linens. If you don't want to worry about shipping, look over the assortment of books, toys and clothing here and in the baby store across the street.
✉ **3548 Sacramento St** ☎ **563-0773** 🚌 **1**
🕐 **Mon-Fri 10am-6pm, Sat 10am-5:30pm, Sun noon-5pm**

Target (1, C2)
This is the discount chain for soccer moms and other parents who appreciate a little style served up alongside with value. It's home base of the baby gift registry (and other things for Mom or Dad like a Michael Graves alarm clock).
✉ **5001 Junipero Serra Blvd, Colma** ☎ **650-992-8433** 🚌 **I-280 south of San Francisco**

to Serramonte Blvd exit, left on Serramonte and under the freeway to corner of Junipero Serra Blvd 🕐 **Mon-Sat 8am-11pm, Sun 8am-10pm**

Tuffy's Hopscotch
(3, D5) Shoes take center stage at this clothing store for children, from tiny sneakers from all the big names in all the hot styles to a fantastic selection of girly-girl sandals that will make any Presidio Heights mother proud.
✉ **3307 Sacramento St** ☎ **440-7599** 🚌 **1, 43**
🕐 **Mon-Sat 10am-5:30pm**

San Francisco Centre

SPECIALTY STORES

Bauerware (6, C2)
Come here for high-design hardware for houses, from drawer handles and pulls to hinges. Spruce up a kitchen, a bathroom or the front door of your house with something you can stash in your carry-on.
✉ 3886 17th St
☎ 864-3886
Ⓜ Muni Castro
🚌 24 ⏰ Mon-Sat 10am-6pm

Bell'occio (6, A4)
Perfumes, antique linens and other reminders of the refinement of life in France are here, in a lovely shop on a rough alley off Market St. (The contrast is part of the appeal.)
✉ 8 Brady St ☎ 864-4048 Ⓜ Muni Van Ness
🚌 5, 6, 7, 66, 71
⏰ Tues-Sat 11am-5pm

Bloomers (4, E1)
There are flower shops and stands all over San Francisco, but none matches Bloomers, from the quality of the blooms to the elegance of accessories such as river rocks (for vases) and real French ribbon (for just about anything).
✉ 2975 Washington St
☎ 563-3266 🚌 1, 24
⏰ Mon-Fri 9am-5pm, Sat 9am-4pm

CompUSA (5, J5)
Check your emails or check the latest gadgets and software at the Wal-Mart of the computer world. A broad selection and good prices compensate for the difficulty in finding a sales clerk to help navigate the options.
✉ 750 Market St

☎ 391-9778 Ⓜ Powell
🚌 5, 6, 7, 21, 66, 71
⏰ Mon-Fri 9am-8pm, Sat 10am-7pm, Sun 11am-6pm

Forrest Jones (3, D5)
This is something like a small-town general store, if the small town were a cozy little village like Pacific Heights and the main business of that little village was entertaining. Find everything for the kitchen and table, plus an eclectic collection of other things people need and use like baskets and umbrellas.
✉ 3274 Sacramento St
☎ 567-2483 🚌 1, 43
⏰ Mon-Sat 10am-6pm, Sun 11am-5pm

George (4, E5)
Is George a gift shop for dogs and cats that also stocks essential items like food and flea preparations, or is it a pet shop with an extraordinary selection of gifts? Visit George here or on Fourth St in Berkeley (1829 Fourth St; 7, B1; ☎ 510-644-1033) and decide.
✉ 2411 California St
☎ 441-0564 🚌 1, 22
⏰ Mon-Fri 11am-6pm,

Sat 10am-6pm, Sun noon-6pm

Lombardi Sports (4, D5) This locally owned sporting-goods store has the right stuff for all the local sports with the possible exception of surfing. There are shoes for runners, suits and goggles for swimmers, equipment from bikes to canoes, kayaks and camping gear, and a staff who can even answer questions.
✉ 1600 Jackson St
☎ 771-0600 🚌 19, 47, 49 ⏰ Mon-Wed 10am-7pm, Thurs-Fri 10am-8pm, Sat & Sun 10am-6pm

Mask Italia (4, B2)
Handmade masks from Italy in traditional commedia dell'arte styles and modern variations are the theme here, with a few feather boas and such to round out a costume for Mardi Gras or Halloween or Carnival in Venice. Astounding styles. Astonishing craftsmanship.
✉ 2176 Chestnut St
☎ 409-4743 🚌 30
⏰ 10am-8pm

Pots & Pans

Chuck Williams is to the kitchenware business what Alice Waters is to food. **Williams-Sonoma** started in a hardware store in Sonoma and moved down to the city in the 1960s. Now it has hundreds of branches across the country, including the Union Square location (150 Post St; 5, H5; ☎ 362-6904). The local cognoscenti also shop at **Sur La Table** downtown (77 Maiden Ln; 5, J5; ☎ 732-7900) and off Fourth St in Berkeley (1806 Forest St; 7, A1; ☎ 510-849-2252).

places to eat

People came to San Francisco to eat long before there were celebrity chefs on every corner. Fresh ingredients were readily available – an extraordinary range and amount of America's produce is grown within a few hours of the city – and cooks from France, Italy and China were available, too, to work with those ingredients.

Today there *are* celebrity chefs on every corner. Dining out is the primary entertainment in town and the secondary topic of conversation after real estate. There are more restaurants here per capita than anywhere else in the country, one for every three or four hundred people at last count. With all this competition and all this talk, bad restaurants don't survive.

It's still a little easier to get a bad meal here than it is in France, but you can get a good French meal, or Thai or Mexican at dozens of places, for a lot less money than you'd pay in London or New York. For sheer depth and breadth of dining choices, San Francisco holds its own with any city in the world.

How Much?

The symbols used in this chapter indicate the cost of a main course, without drinks, tax or tip:

$	main courses under $11
$$	mains $12-17
$$$	mains $18-24
$$$$	mains over $25

Tomasso's, a North Beach pizzeria

Drinks

Most restaurants serve alcoholic drinks (the drinking age is 21; lots of places ask for ID), and most restaurants will serve house wines or a selection of wines by glass. Wines by the glass are usually better quality. Just watch the prices. You'll find a decent selection of beers most places, a great selection in a few. The tap water is safe and delicious. Just ask for 'Hetch-Hetchy' (the name of the city reservoir in the Sierras).

Tipping

As elsewhere in the US, tipping is customary in restaurants. Servers expect 15-20% of the check total before tax. Give a little more if the service was exceptional and a little less if it wasn't. Many restaurants add a service charge for parties of six or more. If you're traveling with a gang, check the check before you tip. Tipping is optional at coffee bars and places where you place your own order at the counter. Fifty cents or a dollar is in order if you ask for something complicated like a double half-caff latte with nonfat soy milk.

Opening Hours

Most places to eat are open seven days a week. Sunday nights and Mondays are the usual closing days for those places that do close. Specific restaurant opening hours are listed in the reviews that follow in this chapter.

Meal Times

Californians tend to start their days early, to get East Coast phone calls out of the way and get home in time for a run before dark. People have breakfast anywhere between 6am and 9am, either at home or near work. Lunch hour starts at noon, the dinner hour about 7pm or 7:30pm. Not many places are open past 10pm during the week or past 11pm on weekends.

Booking Tables

Most but not all moderate to high priced restaurants ($$ and up) take reservations for both lunch and dinner, so call ahead if you can. Many restaurants that take reservations also set seats aside for walk-ins, so do not hesitate to ask. Restaurants that don't take reservations frequently subject customers to long waits (20 minutes or more) so ease into it or find another place.

Watch the North Beach action from Enrico's Sidewalk Café, 504 Broadway.

BERKELEY & OAKLAND

Cafe Rouge
(7, A1) $$$
French
That's *rouge* as in red as in red meat, in all kinds of cuts and forms, prepared and presented with that Chez Panisse/Zuni Cafe left-wing elegant panache. There are other items on the menu for the fish-and-chicken set, all good, but this is a bad place for a vegetarian.
⊠ 1782 4th St, Berkeley
☎ 510-525-1440
🚇 I-80 over Bay Bridge to University Ave exit, continue on frontage road to Hearst St, right on Hearst to 4th St
🕐 lunch 11:30-3pm, dinner Tues-Sat 5:30-10pm, Sun 5-10pm (bar food available in between) ♿

Chez Panisse
(7, A4) $$$$
Californian
If California cuisine has a home, this is it. The revolutionary idea that Americans could use local produce to cook like the French has produced something distinctive (think fresh goat cheese pizza, lobster in yellow tomato broth). Prix fixe downstairs, your choice in the less formal cafe upstairs. Reservations essential.
⊠ 1517 Shattuck Ave, Berkeley ☎ 510-548-5525 🅜 Downtown Berkeley BART 🕐 cafe Mon-Thurs 11:30am-3pm, 5-10:30pm; Fri & Sat 11:30am-3:30pm, 5-11:30pm; downstairs dinner seatings Mon-Sat 6pm & 8:30pm ⓥ

O Chame (7, A1) $
Japanese
The perfect sidewalk cafe for 4th St. Delicate dishes of soba or udon noodles, fusion fare like grilled salmon, served with exquisite style inside or out.
⊠ 1830 4th St, Berkeley ☎ 510-841-8783 🚇 I-80 over Bay Bridge to University Ave exit, continue on frontage road to Hearst St, right on Hearst to 4th St 🕐 lunch Mon-Sat 11:30am-3pm, dinner Mon-Fri ♿ ⓥ

Oliveto (7, A5) $$$$
Northern Italian
Paul Bertolli was the chef at Chez Panisse for over a decade. His cafe and restaurant at Market Hall present Northern Italian food with attention and affection, from pizzas downstairs to special truffle nights upstairs.
⊠ 5655 College Ave, Oakland ☎ 510-547-5356 🅜 Rockridge BART 🕐 cafe Mon-Sat 11:30am-10pm, Sun noon-9pm, restaurant lunch Mon-Fri 11:30am-2pm, dinner Mon-Sat 5:30-10pm, Sun 5-9pm ⓥ

What Is California Cuisine?

The debate over the definition of 'California cuisine' is as complicated as the debate over American identity. Most foodies would agree that CC is based on Californian products prepared with Mediterranean (usually French and Italian) techniques, heavy on the olive oil and veggies, light on the butter and cream. Locals know it when they see it. Visitors from Australia may recognize it as the first cousin of Mod-Oz.

Anthony Pidgeon

THE CASTRO & UPPER MARKET

Blue (6, C2) $
American
A reliable neighborhood restaurant where you can count on the burger or their take on Caesar salad, and you can also count on a bubbly crowd around you.
✉ **2337 Market St**
☎ **863-2583 Ⓜ Muni Castro 🚌 24**
🕐 **11:30am-11pm** Ⓥ

Chow (6, B2) $
American
People line up here and at Park Chow out in the Sunset (1240 9th Ave; 2, E7; ☎ 665-9912) for simple-but-hearty noodle dishes (Italian American and Asian American), equally hearty meat-and-veg dishes (roast chicken, flatiron steak), and all-American fountain items (malteds, shakes, slices of cake the size of a house). Great atmosphere, great value.
✉ **215 Church St**
☎ **552-2469 Ⓜ Muni Castro 🚌 22** 🕐 **Sun-Thurs 11am-11pm, Fri & Sat 11am-midnight** 🚻 Ⓥ

Destino (6, A3) $
South American
Come in for drinks at the bar where the scene is a lively mix of Mission straight and Upper Market gay. Save room for tapas with the taste of Peru, spicy ceviches or tender *anticuchos de cordero* (skewered marinated bites of lamb).
✉ **1815 Market St**
☎ **552-4451 Ⓜ Muni Van Ness or Church 🚌 22**
🕐 **Mon-Sat 5-10pm** 🚻

Firewood Cafe (6, C1) $
Italian
Roast chicken and pizza are the stars on the menu here, smoky from the wood burning oven. Worth standing in the line to place your order, either here or at the branches on Union Square (233 Geary St; 5, J4; ☎ 788-3473) and inside the Metreon (101 4th St; 5, K5; ☎ 369-6299).
✉ **4248 17th St**
☎ **252-0999 Ⓜ Muni Castro 🚌 33, 24**
🕐 **Mon-Thurs 11am-10:30pm, Fri & Sat 11am-11pm, Sun 11am-10pm** 🚻

Home (6, B2) $
American
Cocktails and home cooking with a haute-cuisine edge, from a chef and crew who can turn out fancy stuff at simple prices. Not great for large parties because of the noise.
✉ **2100 Market St**
☎ **503-0333 Ⓜ Muni Church 🚌 22** 🕐 **Sun-Wed 5:30-10pm, Thurs-Sat 5:30-11pm** Ⓥ

Tin-Pan Asian Bistro (6, C2) $$
Fusion
A happy exception to the general rule that fusion cooking does not work. From tea smoked duck flatbread to Singapore shrimp, flavors from the East are blended gracefully with ingredients or techniques from the West.
✉ **2251 Market St**
☎ **565-0733 Ⓜ Muni Castro 🚌 22, 24**
🕐 **Mon-Thurs 11am-11pm, Fri 11am-midnight, Sat 10am-midnight, Sun 10am-11pm** Ⓥ

At Home in the Castro

CHINATOWN

Dol Ho (5, F4) $
Chinese
Chinatown dim sum, a little quieter, a little easier than around the corner at Gold Mountain. The rice crepes with shrimp and other fillings are signature dishes, but just about everything you choose will hit the spot.
✉ 808 Pacific St
☎ 392-2828 🚌 30, 41, 45 ⏰ 7am-5pm ♿ V

Gold Mountain (5, E4) $
Chinese
This is dim sum the way you'd expect to experience it in Hong Kong: fleets of carts working their way through the noise and crowds loaded with sights and smells of dozens of different dishes.
✉ 644 Broadway
☎ 296-7733 🚌 15, 30, 41, 45 ⏰ Mon-Fri 10:30am-3pm, Sat &
Sun 8am-3pm, dinner 5-9:30pm ♿ V

House of Nanking (5, F5) $
Chinese
Nondescript and utilitarian even by Chinatown standards, where customers tend to calculate how much that new clock on the wall is costing them. Great versions of standbys like pot stickers and mu shu pork, at great prices, served with great efficiency. Cash only.
✉ 919 Kearny St
☎ 421-1429 Ⓜ Montgomery 🚌 1, 15, 41 ⏰ Mon-Fri 11am-10pm, Sat noon-1pm, Sun noon-4pm ♿ V

R & G Lounge (5, G5) $
Chinese
This is where local Chinese in the restaurant business go when they have a hankering for Cantonese. Try the roast salt & pepper prawns or beef brisket in a clay pot or something simple like tender chicken with snow peas.
✉ 631 Kearny St
☎ 982-7877 🚌 1, 15 ⏰ Mon-Thurs 10:30am-9:30pm, Fri 10:30am-10pm, Sat 11:30am-10:30pm, Sun 11:30am-9:30pm ♿ V

Yuet Lee (5, E4) $
Chinese
A longtime favorite of San Francisco food mafiosi who claim this is the best Chinese seafood joint in town. It is certainly the best Chinese seafood joint in town that's open to 3 in the morning. Cash only, so be prepared.
✉ 1300 Stockton St
☎ 982-6020 🚌 15, 30, 41, 45 ⏰ Wed-Sun 11am-3am ♿ V

Dig into Dim Sum

Whether you call it 'yum cha' (drink tea) as they do in Hong Kong or Melbourne, or 'dim sum' (little treasures) as they do here, the little bites of steamed dumplings, pastries, rice noodles and more are Great Treasures of world cooking. Just sit as carts loaded with different dishes roll by, and point at whatever you'd like. Our favorite is **Yank Sing** (p. 75). Close contenders include **Ton Kiang** in the Richmond District (5821 Geary Blvd; 2, B5; ☎ 387-8275), which serves dim sum all day, and **Gold Mountain** (p. 72), for the full-on Chinatown experience.

Anthony Pidgeon

CIVIC CENTER & HAYES VALLEY

Absinthe (4, G5) $$$
French
The look and feel of the room and the look and taste of the food on the plates are so French you
have to remind yourself that chef Ross Browne is a New Zealander and that you are in San Francisco.
✉ 398 Hayes St
☎ 551-1590 🚌 21
⏰ Tues-Fri 11:30am-midnight, Sat 10:30am-midnight, Sun 10:30am-10:30pm (bar open to 2am except Sun) V

Absinthe makes the heart grow fonder.

Citizen Cake (4, G5) $$
Californian
Baker Elizabeth Falkner is a lapsed art student whose fanciful cakes and cookies bear the stamp of a woman weaned on Abstract Expressionists. The light meals from chef Jennifer Cox are sure-footed interpretations of French classics, like a winter salad of baby spinach, pancetta and poached egg.
✉ 399 Grove St
☎ 861-2228 Ⓜ Muni Van Ness 🚌 5, 21, 47, 49 ⏰ Tues-Fri 8am-10pm, Sat 10am-10pm, Sun 10am-9pm ♿ Ⓥ

Hayes St Grill
(4, G5) $$$
Seafood
Proprietor Patricia Unterman doubles as a writer and food critic when she's not here or around the corner at Vicolo Pizzeria. Fresh seafood without frou-frou, prepared the way you want it, served with your choice of sauces and sides. Daily specials and such are available for the fish-phobic.
✉ 320 Hayes St ☎ 863-5545 Ⓜ Muni Van Ness 🚌 21, 47, 49 ⏰ lunch Mon-Fri 11:30am-2pm, dinner Mon-Thurs 5-9:30pm, Fri 5-10:30pm, Sat 5:30-10:30pm, Sun 5-8:30pm ♿ Ⓥ

Max's Opera Cafe
(4, G5) $
Delicatessen
San Francisco's answer to a Jewish delicatessen. Good corned beef and good pastrami, on corn rye with your choice of mustards and pickles. Since this is San Francisco, there are salads, other sandwiches and hot dishes, and performances by the wait staff (it's not the Opera Cafe for nothing).
✉ Opera Plaza, 601 Van Ness Ave ☎ 771-7300 Ⓜ Muni Van Ness 🚌 5, 47, 49 ⏰ Sun-Mon 11:30am-10pm, Tues-Thurs 11:30am-11pm, Fri & Sat 11am-midnight ♿ Ⓥ

Powell's Place
(4, H4) $
soul food
Before the freeway to Franklin St came down and the Prada shoes arrived, the west end of Hayes Valley was a quiet African American backwater. Powell's Place is a survivor of that quieter time, serving up fried chicken, corn muffins and collard greens at pre-gentrification prices.
✉ 511 Hayes St
☎ 863-1404 🚌 21 ⏰ 9am-11pm ♿

Stars (4, G5) $$$$
Californian
One of the liveliest dining rooms in the city, especially before performances at the Opera House or Symphony Hall down the street. Grab a snack at the bar or dine on a range of California-style dishes with an Eastern Mediterranean (as opposed to Western Mediterranean) accent.
✉ 555 Golden Gate Ave ☎ 861-7827 Ⓜ Civic Center, Muni Van Ness 🚌 5, 47, 49 ⏰ Mon-Fri 11:30am-midnight, Sat & Sun 5pm-midnight Ⓥ

Terra Brazilis
(4, H4) $$
Brazilian
Traditional dishes (*feijoada*, Bahia chicken and rock shrimp sauté, lamb sirloin) with traditional flavors of citrus, spice and coconut oil adapted by a Californian chef for Californians used to eating a little lighter than Latin Americans do. Elegant and fun.
✉ 602 Hayes St
☎ 241-1900 🚌 21 ⏰ Tues-Thurs 11:30am-9:30pm, Fri & Sat 5:30-10:30pm ♿ Ⓥ

Zuni Cafe (4, H5) $$$
Mediterranean
Like Rick's in Casablanca, everyone comes to Zuni. The long copper bar and two floors of dining rooms hum like a great Parisian brasserie on a Saturday night. Signature dishes include roast chicken for two fresh from the brick oven or oysters fresh from the oyster bar.
✉ 1658 Market St
☎ 552-2522 Ⓜ Muni Van Ness 🚌 6, 7, 66, 71 ⏰ Tues-Sat 11:30am-midnight, Sun 11am-11pm ♿ Ⓥ

FINANCIAL DISTRICT

Aqua (5, G6) $$$$
Seafood
Wonderful if sometimes overwrought seafood dishes (black mussel soufflé, citrus steamed Thai snapper, roasted monkfish, to name a few) in a dining room austere enough to satisfy Armani or Jil Sandler. Power lunching, power drinks, power dining.
✉ 252 California St
☎ 956-9662 Ⓜ Embarcadero, California cable car 🚌 1, 2, 3, 4 🕐 lunch Mon-Fri 11:30am-2pm, dinner Mon-Thurs 5-9:30pm, Fri & Sat 5-10:30pm

B-44 (5, H5) $$
Catalan
A Catalan bistro that serves eight kinds of paella and a list of main courses from salt cod and roast rabbit to a chicken and monkfish combo dubbed the 'mar/muntanya.' Not a good place for business, because it's too noisy and too much fun.
✉ 44 Belden Pl ☎ 986-6287 Ⓜ Montgomery 🚌 15, 30, 45 🕐 lunch Mon-Fri 11:30am-2:30pm, dinner Mon-Sat 5:30pm-midnight Ⓥ

Escape from New York Pizza (5, H5) $
Pizzeria
When you just want to grab and go, EFNY has tasty slices (from pepperoni to feta cheese with fresh spinach) ready in a flash, and a modest assortment of salads. Also located in the Castro (508 Castro St; 6, D1; ☎ 252-1515) and the Haight (1737 Haight St; 2, D9; ☎ 668-5577)
✉ 333 Bush St ☎ 421-0700 Ⓜ Montgomery

🚌 15, 45 🕐 Mon-Fri 9am-6pm, Sat 11am-3pm ♿ Ⓥ

Harbor Village (5, F7) $$
Chinese
Chinese food with a view, serving dim sum at lunch and sensational Cantonese and seafood dishes in the evenings (the Harbor Village people have a couple of restaurants on the water back in Kowloon, so they're old hands at this).
✉ 4 Embarcadero Center ☎ 781-8833 Ⓜ Embarcadero, California cable car 🚌 1, 41 🕐 lunch Mon-Fri 11am-2:30pm, Sat & Sun 10:30am-2:30pm, dinner 5:30-9:30pm ♿ Ⓥ

Harrington's Bar & Grill (5, G6) $
American
They don't do St Patrick's Day here anymore. It got to be much too hard. The rest of the year this is as authentically San Francisco–Irish an institution as you'll find anywhere. Two good bars, a smoking patio for smokers and bar food like burgers and hot beef sandwiches.
✉ 245 Front St ☎ 392-7595 Ⓜ Embarcadero,

California cable car
🚌 1, 41 🕐 Mon-Sat 10:30am-9pm

Palio Paninoteca (5, G5) $
Italian
Come here for low-cost sandwiches (some grilled at your option, some cold), fresh salads and daily pasta and soup specials to warm your bones on cold days. Also located at UCSF Medical Center (500 Parnassus Ave; 2, E8; ☎ 681-9925).
✉ 505 Montgomery St ☎ 362-6900 Ⓜ Montgomery 🚌 1, 10, 15 🕐 Mon-Fri 6:30am-4pm ♿ Ⓥ

Plouf (5, H5) $$
French Seafood
'Plouf' is French for 'splash' and Plouf has made a splash in the Financial District with mussels eight ways, other French-inflected seafood dishes, and pasta and meat for the die-hards. Enjoy inside or out of doors under blue skies in Belden Place.
✉ 40 Belden Pl ☎ 986-6491 Ⓜ Montgomery, California cable car 🚌 2, 3, 4 🕐 Mon-Sat 11am-10:30pm

Belden Place, San Francisco's European Quarter

Rubicon (5, G5)   **$$$$**
French-Californian
From the people who brought Nobu and Montrachet to New York comes this fine French restaurant with a Californian edge (try veal chops wrapped in grape leaves or John Dory en papillote). The paneled rooms have the feel of a modern men's club where women are welcome as members.
✉ **558 Sacramento St**
☎ **434-4100**
Ⓜ Montgomery 🚌 **1, 15, 45** ⊘ **lunch Mon-Fri 11:30am-2:30pm, dinner Mon-Sat 5:30-10:30pm** V

Sam's Grill (5, H5) **$$$**
Seafood
Financial District types, their fathers (it was strictly a guy's game then) and their grandfathers have filled the booths at Sam's for simple meals that seemed to define San Francisco – grilled local fish and a green salad, washed down with a drink or a glass of white wine.
✉ **374 Bush St** ☎ **421-0594** Ⓜ **Montgomery**
🚌 **15, 30, 45** ⊘ **Mon-Fri 11am-9pm** ⚥ V

Sorabol (5, G8)   **$**
Korean fusion
The best noodle shop in the Financial District can be jammed at lunch time, so beware. From Japanese-style udon dishes to Hawaiian-style saimin, they serve everything that slurps and well. Solid food, too, if you insist.
✉ **Rincon Center, 101 Spear St** ☎ **896-5959**
Ⓜ **Embarcadero** 🚌 **1, 2, 7, 9, 14, 21, 66, 71** ⊘ **Mon-Fri 10:30am-3:30pm** ⚥ V

Specialties (5, H6)   **$**
American
At last count there were seven branches of Specialties around the Financial District, each serving muffins and bagels in the morning and forty kinds of sandwiches for lunch. They'll do sandwich baskets and lunch boxes if you've got a group to feed al fresco.
✉ **22 Battery St**
☎ **398-4691**

Big Dinner Deals
If you're looking for the Goldilocks business dinner (not too simple, not too expensive, not too quiet, not too dull), try **Aqua** (p. 74), **Rubicon** (p. 75) or **Campton Place** (p. 82).

Ⓜ **Embarcadero** 🚌 **2, 3, 4, 6, 7, 21, 66, 71** ⊘ **Mon-Fri 6am-6pm** ⚥ V

Yank Sing (5, G8)   **$$**
Chinese (dim sum)
The best dim sum in San Francisco, which means some of the best dim sum in the world. A parade of delights from Peking Duck and minced squab in lettuce leaves to simple steamed dumplings. Try them here or nearby at 49 Stevenson St (5, H6, ☎ 541-4949).
✉ **1 Rincon Center, 101 Spear St** ☎ **957-9300** Ⓜ **Embarcadero**
🚌 **1, 2, 7, 9, 14, 21, 66, 71** ⊘ **Mon-Fri 11am-3pm, Sat, Sun & holidays 10am-4pm** ⚥ V

HAIGHT-ASHBURY

Cha Cha Cha (2, D9)   **$$**
Caribbean
This tapas bar is a clearing house for the straight single set for the area between the Castro and the University of San Francisco. Tropical drinks and sangria flowing at the bar go with the little dishes drawn from Mexico and the Islands on the tables.
✉ **1801 Haight St**
☎ **386-7670** Ⓜ **Muni N line** 🚌 **6, 7, 43, 66, 71** ⊘ **lunch 11:30am-4pm, dinner 5-11pm**

EOS Restaurant & Wine Bar (2, D9) **$$$**
Fusion
Some of the best fusion cooking in San Francisco is on this back street on the edge of the Haight. Try tangerine peel braised osso bucco, or perhaps the tea smoked duck breast with mashed potatoes. Or simply come for an adventure at the wine bar.
✉ **901 Carl St** ☎ **566-3063** Ⓜ **Muni N line**
🚌 **43** ⊘ **Sun-Thurs 5:30-10pm, Fri 5:30-11pm** V

Indian Oven (3, E7)   **$**
Indian
Tandoori dishes draw people here from all over San Francisco, where they wait patiently for their chance to taste chicken *tikka, boti kehbab* or the mixed tandoori special. There's a full assortment of other dishes to boot, some with meat and many without.
✉ **233 Fillmore St**
☎ **626-1628** Ⓜ **Muni J or N lines** 🚌 **6, 7, 22, 66, 71** ⊘ **5-11pm** ⚥ V

Indian Oven, Tandoori goodness in the Haight

Rosamunde Grill
(3, E7) **$**
Sausages
In a city with designer pizzas it's no surprise to find a designer sausage stand, with German wursts from knocks to bocks and other varieties like *merguez* and chicken curry. Grilled to perfection in front of you, washed down with Thomas Kemper sodas or beer from Toronado next door.
✉ **545 Haight St**
☎ **437-6851** Ⓜ **Muni J or N lines** 🚌 **6, 7, 22, 66, 71** ⏲ **11:30am-10pm** ♿

Thep Phanom (3, E7) $
Thai
This is one of the best regarded Thai restaurants around, which explains the waiting list if you didn't call ahead. Everyone loves the *tom yum gai* (chicken soup with lemongrass and veggies), but you could choose blind and dine happily.
✉ **400 Waller St**
☎ **431-2526** Ⓜ **Muni J or N lines** 🚌 **6, 7, 22, 66, 71** ⏲ **5:30-10:30pm** ♿ Ⓥ

JAPANTOWN

Mifune (4, F3) $
Japanese
Best noodle shop in the Japan Center, with combinations you won't see in other restaurants. Try the udon (fat white wheat noodles) or the soba (brown thin buckwheat noodles) hot or cold, with anything from seaweeds to fish cakes.
✉ **Kintetsu Mall, 1737 Post St** ☎ **922-0337** 🚌 **2, 3, 4, 38** ⏲ **Sun-Thurs 11am-9:30pm, Fri & Sat 11am-10pm** ♿ Ⓥ

On the Bridge
(4, F3) **$**
Japanese fusion
Japanese food isn't all raw fish and noodle soups. Curry arrived in Japan centuries ago, some say with Buddhists from India. Pastas arrived more recently, with the Europeans who started putting down stakes there in the 19th century. Tastes from these traditions fill the menu here.
✉ **Japan Center, 1581 Webster St** ☎ **931-2743** 🚌 **2, 3, 4, 38** ⏲ **11:30am-10pm** ♿ Ⓥ

Mifune, Japantown gem

MISSION DISTRICT

Burger Joint (6, D4) $
Burgers
A retro-vision of a burger joint from the sixties, serving local Niman Ranch beef burgers, grilled chicken breasts and hot dogs (for kids, it seems), with great fries, great shakes and decent music on the box. Also located in the Lower Haight (700 Haight St; 6, A1; ☎ 864-3833)
✉ 807 Valencia St
☎ 824-3494 🚌 33, 26, 49 ⏰ 11am-11pm ♿

Delfina (6, C4) $$$
Mediterranean
They say 'Don't Be Afraid of Your Food' and they mean it. Craig Stoll has instinctive feel for Mediterranean cooking that comes to the table embodied in a salt cod brandade or a small plate of grilled calamari with a white bean salad, without attitude or crazy prices.
✉ 3621 18th St
☎ 552-4055 Ⓜ Muni J line 🚌 22, 33
⏰ Sun-Thurs 5:30-10pm, Fri & Sat 5:30-11pm Ⓥ

Gordon's House of Fine Eats (3, F8) $$$
Modern American
If you want a picture of San Francisco during the dot-com boom, try Gordon's for comfort (pizza, matzo ball soup), luxury (dayboat scallops, lamb t-bones) or fusion food (asparagus eggrolls anyone?). Part restaurant, part gallery, part music hall with performances five nights a week. Lively, tasty, noisy and expensive.
✉ 500 Florida St
☎ 861-8900 🚌 27, 33

⏰ lunch Mon-Fri 11:30am-4:30pm, dinner Sun-Mon 5:30-10pm, Tues-Wed 5:30-11pm, Thurs-Sat 5:30-midnight Ⓥ

Herbivore (6, D4) $
Vegetarian
These people make their restaurant and their food so clean and fresh and lovely to look at that even confirmed carnivores have been known to drift in and give the Herbivore's selection of vegan and vegetarian dishes a try.
✉ 983 Valencia St
☎ 826-5657 🚌 14, 26, 49 ⏰ Sun-Thurs 11am-10pm, Fri & Sat 11am-11pm ♿ Ⓥ

La Taqueria (6, F5) $
Mexican
Simply the best taqueria in San Francisco. For twice the price of a meal at Taco Bell, you can have a soft taco at La Taqueria filled with freshly grilled meats, savory carnitas (shredded pork) or chicken. If they only had rice for the burritos life would be perfect.
✉ 2889 Mission St
☎ 285-7117 Ⓜ 24th St BART 🚌 14, 48, 49
⏰ Mon-Sat 11am-9pm Sun 11am-8pm ♿ Ⓥ

Mangiafuoco (6, C4) $$
Italian
The name means 'fire eater' in Italian, but don't worry about heartburn. The pasta dishes and traditional *secondi* of meat or fish are light, fresh and luscious. Want something more innovative? Try the *pesce* for two (a sauté of fish and seafood and vegetables) or *mezzelune* with squash.
✉ 1001 Guerrero St
☎ 206-9881 🚌 26
⏰ Sun, Mon, Wed & Thurs 5:30-10pm, Fri & Sat 5:30-11pm Ⓥ

Pauline's Pizza (6, B4) $
Pizzeria
This is the home of designer pizza in San Francisco, with crusts as thin as a fashion model dressed up with toppings such as chicken sausage, Louisiana andouille or thin-sliced potatoes with green olives. Ready for its closeup . . .
✉ 260 Valencia St
☎ 552-2050 Ⓜ 16th St BART 🚌 14, 26, 49
⏰ Tues-Sat 5-10pm ♿ Ⓥ

Slanted Door (6, C4) $$
Vietnamese Fusion
The inheritance from France and China range from stir

After Hours
Several restaurants around the Civic Center stay open until midnight, particularly when something is playing at the Opera House or Davies Symphony Hall. Options include **Stars** (555 Golden Gate Ave), **Absinthe** (p. 72) and **Zuni Cafe** (p. 73). For late-late, try **Yuet Lee** in Chinatown, open to 3am (p. 72) or **Mel's Drive In** (p. 80) and the **Bagdad Cafe** (2295 Market St, ☎ 621-4434), which never close.

Foreign Cinema (p. 41)

fry mains to elegant desserts, with California touches like a jicama & grapefruit salad starter, in the best Vietnamese restaurant in America. In temporary quarters at 100 Brannan St (5, K8) through May 2003 while remodeling Valencia St. Reservations essential for dinner.
✉ **584 Valencia St**
☎ **861-8032** Ⓜ **16th St BART** 🚌 **14, 22, 26, 49** ⏰ **Tues-Sun lunch 11:30am-3pm, dinner 5:30-10pm** ♿ **V**

Slow Club (3, F8)   **$$**
American
Twenty-first century

American food (Caesar salads, burgers, grilled salmon, roast chicken with mashed potatoes) in a zippy room that started life as a bar and morphed into a restaurant because the bar food was so good.
✉ **2501 Mariposa St**
☎ **241-9390** 🚌 **9, 27, 33** ⏰ **lunch Mon-Fri 11:30-2:30pm, brunch Sat & Sun 10am-2:30pm, dinner Mon-Thurs 6:30-10pm, Fri & Sat 6:30-11pm** **V**

Taqueria Pancho Villa (6, C4)   **$**
Mexican
The best burrito in town, with apologies to La Taqueria. Start with a flour tortilla and rice, choose between three kinds of beans and meats from carnitas to shrimp to tofu. Watch them roll it up together, then choose one of the half-dozen salsas for the final touch.
✉ **3071 16th St**
☎ **864-8840** Ⓜ **16th St BART** 🚌 **14, 22, 26, 49** ⏰ **10am-midnight** ♿ **V**

Tokyo Go Go (6, B4)   **$$**
Japanese
The hip spot for sushi on the hip strip of 16th St, serving the raw stuff the way you like it and hot food both classic (*onigiri*, traditional rice balls) and contemporary (steamed mussels in sake sauce).
✉ **3174 16th St**
☎ **864-2288** Ⓜ **16th St BART** 🚌 **14, 22, 26, 49** ⏰ **Tues-Thur 5:30-10:30pm, Fri & Sat 5:30-11pm, Sun 5-10pm** **V**

Universal Cafe (3, F8)   **$$$**
Modern American
Something for everyone here. Brunch on salads or sandwiches inside or out at four tables for sidewalk dining. Dine on Mediterranean-inflected dishes from flatbreads to grilled meats at night. Enjoy the industrial chic atmosphere any time.
✉ **2814 19th St**
☎ **821-4608** 🚌 **27** ⏰ **brunch 9am-2:30pm Sat & Sun, dinner Sun-Thurs 5:30-10pm, Fri & Sat 5:30-11pm** **V**

NOE VALLEY

Firefly (6, F1)   **$$**
Modern American
Not every innovation on the menu works, but where else can you find a wild mushroom enchilada or grilled tuna with soba noodles? Look for the giant firefly in front.
✉ **4288 24th St**
☎ **821-7652** Ⓜ **Muni J line** 🚌 **24, 48** ⏰ **5:30-9:30pm** **V**

Hamano Sushi (6, F1)   **$$**
Japanese
This neighborhood spot is

on all the short lists for sushi, which explains the wait for seats at the sushi bar that start early every evening. Hamano Sushi also serves a full line of hot dishes, from noodles to tempura to that American standby, the sushi-teriyaki combination.
✉ **1332 Castro St**
☎ **826-0825** Ⓜ **Muni J line** 🚌 **24, 48** ⏰ **Sun 5:30-9:30pm, Mon 6-9pm, Tues-Sat 5:30-10:30pm** ♿ **V**

> ## Dining with Kids
> Chinese restaurants are great for kids. Everyone gets what they want with dim sum, and people are used to eating family-style. If your kids are foreign-food-phobic, find kid-friendly food courts at the **Rincon Center** (p. 33), along **Justin Herman Plaza** (p. 40), and in **San Francisco Centre** (p. 56).

NORTH BEACH

Helmand (5, E5) **$$**
Afghan
The best Afghan restaurant in the city sits like a well-dressed matron amid the strip clubs on Broadway. Taste the lamb dishes or the sweet pumpkin with yogurt sauce to see how Afghan food borrows flavors from the Levant and India.
✉ 430 Broadway
☎ 362-0641 🚌 15, 30, 41, 45 ⊙ Tues-Thurs 5:30-10pm, Fri & Sat 5:30-11pm ♿ **V**

Malvina (5, E4) **$**
Italian
Sit in the windows looking over Union St and Washington Square, nibble at your omelet or your sandwich on fresh focaccia bread, and watch the world go by. Easier and quieter than Mama's on the next corner, and just as good.
✉ 1600 Stockton St
☎ 391-1290 🚌 15, 30, 41, 45 ⊙ Mon-Sat 7am-5pm, Sun 8am-4pm ♿ **V**

Mario's Bohemian Cigar Store Cafe (5, E3) **$**
Italian
This is a bar with a grill that turns out sensational Italian-inspired sandwiches on focaccia bread. Our favorites are the meatballs and the eggplant; you might prefer one of their salads or polenta dishes. Also on Russian Hill at 2209 Polk St (4, C5, ☎ 776-8226).
✉ 566 Columbus Ave
☎ 362-0536 🚌 15, 30, 39, 41, 45 ⊙ 10am-midnight ♿ **V**

Rose Pistola (5, E4) **$$$**
Italian
It's not enough to say 'Northern Italian' these days, you have to specify a region, in this case Liguria. You'll find Ligurian dishes on the menu and Californian dishes with Ligurian style, like a grilled arctic char with potatoes and green garlic, or wafer-thin pizzas with rock shrimp and arugula.
✉ 532 Columbus Ave
☎ 399-0499 🚌 15, 30, 41, 45 ⊙ lunch 11:30am-3pm, dinner Sun-Thurs 5:30-11pm, Fri & Sat 5:30pm-midnight **V**

Tomasso's (5, E5) **$**
Italian
You can smell the wood-burning oven a block away on a good night, calling you with the promise of marvelous pizzas in traditional formats (no Santa Fe BBQ chicken here, please). They also serve conventional pasta dishes, but that's not why you're here.
✉ 1042 Kearny St
☎ 398-9696 🚌 15, 30, 41, 45 ⊙ Tues-Sat 5-10:45pm, Sun 4-9:45pm ♿ **V**

PACIFIC HEIGHTS & MARINA DISTRICT

Balboa Cafe (4, C2) **$$**
American
The corner of Fillmore and Greenwich is called the Bermuda Triangle because so many singles disappear here into the night. Come for the noise and the action or come for the food: solid bar and grill fare like a steak or a piece of fish and a salad.
✉ 3199 Fillmore St
☎ 921-3944 🚌 22, 41, 45 ⊙ Mon-Fri 11:30am-2am, Sat-Sun 11am-2am

Ella's (3, D6) **$**
American
With all the restaurants in the city, food has to be special for people to line up the way they do at Ella's. Famous for breakfast, but equally deft at lunch or dinner with comforts like chicken pot pie or meatloaf your mother never made.
✉ 500 Presidio Ave
☎ 441-5669 🚌 1, 2, 3, 4, 43 ⊙ breakfast Mon-Fri 7-11am, brunch Sat & Sun 8:30am-2pm, lunch & dinner Mon-Fri 11am-9pm ♿ **V**

Elite Cafe (4, E3) **$$$**
Cajun
A re-creation of old New Orleans with an oyster bar in front and private booths in the back, serving faithful renditions of Cajun and Creole classics, from tangy gumbos and jambalayas to fiery blackened redfish. Reservations for six or more only, so prepare to wait.
✉ 2049 Fillmore St
☎ 346-8668 🚌 1, 3, 4, 22 ⊙ Mon-Sat 5-11pm, Sun 5-10pm

Greens (4, A3)   **$$**
Vegetarian
Spectacular vegetarian
fare in a dining room on
the water at Fort Mason.
The view of the marina
next door and Golden Gate
Bridge in the distance
complements the sight
of the food on your plate,
much of it from the Zen
Center's Green Gulch
Ranch in Marin.
✉ **Building A, Fort
Mason Center** ☎ 771-
6222 🚌 22 🕐 **lunch
Tues-Sat 11:30am-2pm,
dinner Mon-Fri 5:30-
9:30, prix fixe dinner**
Sat 5:30-9pm, desserts
Tues-Sat 9:30pm-mid-
night **V**

Mel's Drive-In
(4, C2)   **$**
American
Mel's sits on Lombard as
though it has been here
since the Golden Gate
Bridge was built, but it's
relatively new, which is one
measure of its authenticity.
It serves drive-in standbys
like burgers, malts, fries
and sandwiches, and
serves them 24-7-365,
another one of its virtues.
✉ **2165 Lombard St**
☎ 921-3039 🚌 22, 45
🕐 24-7 ♿ **V**

Pluto's (4, C1)   **$**
American
A carvery/cafeteria for the
21st century. Stand in line
for a choice of salads and
main courses of roast
turkey, roast chicken,
roast beef or sausage
carved to order and
served as hot plates or
sandwiches. Very tasty
and very economical.
✉ **3258 Scott St**
☎ 775-8867 🚌 22, 30
🕐 11:30am-10pm
♿ **V**

POTRERO HILL

Eliza's (3, F9)   **$**
Chinese
One of the nicest and all-
around easiest Chinese
restaurants outside of
downtown or Chinatown.
The menu features dishes
from all parts of China,
from sizzling rice soup to
Hunan lamb.
✉ **1457 18th St**
☎ 648-9999 🚌 22
🕐 **Mon-Fri 11am-3pm,
5-9:45pm, Sat 11am-
9:45pm, Sun noon-
9:45pm** ♿ **V**

42 Degrees (3, F10) **$$$**
Californian
Worth a detour for a drink
just to see the industrial-
chic space (designed for
the Esprit people at the
height of their glory), to sit
in the garden and to hear
the live music. Worth staying for roast ox tails, grilled
halibut and other
Californian delights.
✉ **499 Illinois St**
☎ 777-5558 🚌 15
🕐 Wed-Sat 6-10pm **V**

North Star (3, F9)   **$$**
American
Dot-commies who survived
the bust and design people
from the showroom land at
the foot of the hill fill
North Star at lunch for
hearty salads and hot food,
from BBQ pork sandwiches
to fish & chips. Locals fill it
at dinner for similar fare.
✉ **288 Connecticut St**
☎ 551-9840 🚌 22
🕐 lunch Mon-Fri 11:30-
2:30pm, brunch Sat &
Sun 10am-2:30pm, din-
ner Sun-Wed 5:30-
9:30pm, Thurs-Sat 5:30-
10:30pm **V**

Vegetarian Victuals
An extraordinary amount of the produce consumed
in the US is grown within a few hours of the San
Francisco Produce Market, so there's no shortage of
vegetarian restaurants here. Our favorite no-meat
zones include **Greens** (above), **Herbivore** (p. 77),
and **Millennium** (246 McAllister St, ☎ 487-9800).

Anthony Pidgeon

Where's the beef? Not here at the Herbivore.

RUSSIAN HILL

La Folie (4, C5) $$$$
French

Jacques Pepin comes here for dinner when he's filming one of his cooking shows at KQED-TV. Roland Passot's fine French hand is in evidence whether you order a la carte (try the snails or veal chop) or the five-course discovery meal.

✉ 2316 Polk St
☎ 776-5577 🚌 19, 41, 45, 47, 49
🕐 Mon-Sat 5:30-10pm

Swan Oyster Depot (4, D5) $
Seafood

A fish market with a lunch counter with the freshest cracked crabs, oysters and smoked fish in town. Eat at the counter or take away if it's busy (as it usually is). Cash only.

✉ 1517 Polk St
☎ 673-1101 🚊 California cable car 🚌 1, 19, 47, 49 🕐 Mon-Sat 8am-5:30pm ♿

Zarzeula (4, C5) $$
Spanish

A lively local spot with hot and cold running tapas (snails in garlic, chicken croquettes) to keep the hunger at bay while you decide whether to go for the paella for two or a couple of smaller hot dishes for one.

✉ 2000 Hyde St
☎ 346-0800
🚊 Powell-Hyde cable car 🚌 41, 45 🕐 Tues-Sat 5:30-11pm 🇻

SOUTH OF MARKET

Acme Chophouse (5, M9) $$$
American

Traci Des Jardins of Jardiniere has taken on a steakhouse – a steakhouse, no less, at the ballpark in front of the statue of Willie Mays. She's small, but she's up to it. They're cranking out oysters and steaks (some are grass fed – the taste is sensational).

✉ Pacific Bell Park, 24 Willie Mays Plaza
☎ 644-0240 🚊 Muni F line 🚌 10, 15, 30, 45
🕐 game days 10:30am-2:30pm, 4:30-11:30pm; other days 4:30-10:30pm

Bizou (5, M7) $$$
French

You've never had parts the way Loretta Keller presents them, from her signature beef cheeks to pieces of monkfish you didn't know monkfish had. Like the room itself, they're not fancy, just comfortable and satisfying.

✉ 598 4th St ☎ 543-2222 🚌 30, 45 🕐 lunch Mon-Fri 11:30am-

2:30pm, dinner Mon-Thurs 5:30-10pm, Fri & Sat 5:30-10:30pm

AG Ferrari (5, J6) $
Italian delicatessen

The Ferraris started in Oakland, and now have 13 delicatessens around the bay, including this one downtown, one in the Castro (468 Castro St, ☎ 255-6590) and one in Laurel Village (3490 California St, ☎ 923-4470). Get sandwiches and hot meals to eat here or take away to Yerba Buena Gardens.

✉ 688 Mission St
☎ 344-0644
🚊 Montgomery 🚌 14, 15, 30 🕐 Mon-Sat 10am-7:30pm, Sun 11am-6pm ♿ 🇻

Fringale (5, M7) $$$
French

Gerald Hirigoyen's French Basque bistro is so small you could miss it driving down 4th St, but there's no missing the flavors in the food when you sit down. Indelibly French tastes of steamed

mussels or a duck leg with lentils, unmistakably French pastries for dessert. Reservations essential.

✉ 570 4th St ☎ 543-0573 🚌 30, 45 🕐 Mon-Fri 11:30am-3pm, Mon-Sat 5:30-10:30pm

Hawthorne Lane (5, K6) $$$$
Californian

As pretty as they come – from the courtyard off the street to the clean warm dining rooms within historic brick walls. As delicious as they come, fusions by a careful hand, turning out roasted beef carpaccio, grilled venison, seared miso-glazed scallops and more. Reservations essential.

✉ 22 Hawthorne Ln
☎ 777-9779
🚊 Montgomery
🚌 10, 15 🕐 Mon-Fri 11:30am-2pm, Sun-Thurs 5:30-10pm, Fri & Sat 5:30-10:30pm 🇻

Red's Java House (5, J9) $
Burgers

It doesn't get much better

than this. You go down to the Embarcadero, stand in line for a chiliburger and a beer, give them a couple of bucks and take it all outside to eat while you watch the water, the boats and the people going by.

✉ **Pier 30** ☎ 777-5626 Ⓜ **Muni F line** ⏱ Mon-Tues 6am-4pm, Wed-Fri 6am-8pm, Sat 9am-8pm, Sun 9am-3pm ♿

Town's End Restaurant & Bakery (5, L9) $
American
A neighborhood place in

the middle of the new apartments and lofts that make up the new neighborhood of South Beach. Best for breakfast or pastries, a reasonable suggestion for a simple lunch or dinner.

✉ **2 Townsend St** ☎ 512-0749 Ⓜ **Muni F line** ⏱ breakfast Tues-Fri 7:30-11am, brunch Sat & Sun 8am-2:30pm, lunch Tues-Fri 11:30am-2:30pm, dinner Tues-Thurs 5-9pm, Fri & Sat 5-10pm ♿ **V**

XYZ (5, K6) $$$
Californian
The food served at XYZ is at least as stylish as the people running around the lobby of the W Hotel outside. California sturgeon with lobster mashed potatoes adorns plates next to pepper crusted tuna with vegetable hash. The food is a feast for all the senses, every meal of the day.

✉ **W Hotel, 181 3rd St** ☎ 817-7836 Ⓜ Montgomery 🚌 15, 30 ⏱ 6:30-10:30am, 11:30am-3pm, 5:30-10:30pm **V**

UNION SQUARE

Cafe de la Presse (5, H5) $
French
A French-accented cafe serving continental and American breakfast and light lunches and dinners, with dishes like a *croque monsieur* alongside local stuff like hamburger and fries. Great international newsstand if you need something to read while you eat.

✉ **352 Grant Ave** ☎ 398-2680 Ⓜ Montgomery 🚌 2, 3, 4, 15, 30 ⏱ 7am-11pm ♿ **V**

Campton Place (5, H4) $$$$
French
Hailed as one of the best hotel restaurants in the country from the minute it opened 20 years ago, it's still one of the best today. Once American, the food is now French (pepper-coated grouper, for example), with special food and wine pairings for serious gastronomes.

✉ **340 Stockton St**

Outdoor dining on Maiden Lane, off Union Square

☎ 955-5555 Ⓜ Powell 🚌 2, 3, 4, 30 ⏱ breakfast Mon-Fri 7-10:30am, Sat & Sun 8-10:30am, brunch Sun 11am-2pm, lunch Mon-Fri 11:30-2pm, Sat noon-2pm, dinner Mon-Thurs 5:30-10pm, Fri & Sat 5:30-10:30pm, Sun 5:30-9pm **V**

Fleur de Lys (5, H3) $$$$
French
Hubert Keller was trained in the old country and it

shows. Classic French cooking – inventive *oui*, experimental *non*. Impeccably served in a tented dining room that recalls St Laurent's peasant chic phase.

✉ **777 Sutter St** ☎ 673-7779 Ⓜ Powell 🚌 2, 3, 4 ⏱ Mon-Thurs 6:30-9:30pm, Fri & Sat 5:30-10:30pm **V**

Mocca on Maiden Lane (5, J4) $
American
Breakfast and lunch in a Mediterranean key, most

visible in the cold salads at lunch. Nice choice of sandwiches, including a London broil served on a baguette with enough gravy to redefine the term 'French Dip.'
✉ 175 Maiden Ln
☎ 956-1188 Ⓜ Powell
🚌 2, 3, 4, 30, 45
🕐 9:30am-4:30pm ♿ Ⓥ

Sears Fine Food
(5, H4) $
American
This coffee shop has served 'twelve little pancakes' to visitors since some time in the 1930s. Its draw is partly location, amid all the large and small hotels around Union Square, and partly the charm of walking into a modest time warp for an adequate, inexpensive breakfast or lunch.
✉ 439 Powell St
☎ 986-1190 Ⓜ Powell, Powell-Mason & Powell-Hyde cable cars 🚌 2, 3, 4 🕐 6:30am-2:30pm ♿

WATERFRONT

Boulevard
(5, G8) $$$$
Modern American
Tall food and potatoes from Nancy Oakes and restaurant designer Pat Kuleto, whose signature Brothers Grimm touches crowd the room. Glazed quail perched on foie gras toasts, or pan roasted duck breast on corn cakes are representative. Must be seen and tasted to believe. Reservations essential.
✉ Audiffred Bldg, 1 Mission St ☎ 543-6084 Ⓜ Embarcadero, Muni F line 🚌 2, 7, 9, 14, 66, 71 🕐 Mon-Fri 11:30am-2pm, Sun-Wed 5:30-10pm, Thurs-Sat 5:30-10:30pm Ⓥ

Il Fornaio (5, D5) $$
Italian
One of the chain of classy Italian restaurants that dot the better zip codes of the country, this one even better than most because of its stunning space inside an old building at Levi Plaza and its enormous south-facing patio facing the center of the Plaza.
✉ Levi Plaza, 1265 Battery St ☎ 986-0100 Ⓜ Muni F line 🚌 10 🕐 espresso bar Mon-Sat from 7am, Sun from 7:30pm, lunch Mon-Sat 11:30am-2:30pm, brunch Sun 9am-3pm, dinner Sun-Thurs 5-10pm, Fri & Sat 5-11pm Ⓥ

In-N-Out Burger
(5, B1) $
Burgers
The In-N-Out people prove there are alternatives to Mickey D's. Fresh beef, not frozen, French fries fresh-cut from Idaho potatoes. Were that not enough, employee-friendly policies (decent pay, real promotion opportunities, health insurance and other benefits) will make you feel good about eating something so delicious.
✉ 333 Jefferson St
☎ 800-786-1000
Ⓜ Muni F line, Powell-Mason & Powell-Hyde cable cars 🚌 10, 47 🕐 Sun-Thurs 10:30am-1am, Fri & Sat 10:30-1:30am ♿

Waterfront Restaurant & Cafe
(5, E7) $$$
Californian
Usually the better the view, the worse the food. The Waterfront is an exception. Whether you're eating in the casual cafe downstairs or the restaurant above, the fresh fish on your plate will compete for attention with the Bay and the boats out the windows.
✉ Pier 7 ☎ 391-2696 Ⓜ Embarcadero, Muni F line 🚌 12 🕐 cafe Mon-Sat 11:30am-4pm, 5-10pm, Sun 10am-4:30pm, restaurant Mon-Sat 5:30-10pm Ⓥ

Anthony Pidgeon

Room with a View
The **Carnelian Room** on the top of the Bank of America Building (555 California St, ☎ 433-7500) is the *capo di tutti* view restaurant. It's open to the public for drinks or dinner daily from 3pm (plus a Sunday brunch). Runners-up include **The Waterfront** (above), **Harbor Village** (p. 74), **Beach Chalet** (1080 Great Highway, ☎ 386-8439) and of course, **Red's Java House** (p. 81).

entertainment

Hedonism has been part of the San Francisco DNA since the gold rush, so the range of ways one can entertain oneself here is not surprising. From a wonderful array of bars to world-class opera, something is sure to appeal to either the senses or the mind. There's every kind of music at concerts and clubs. There are places to dance to all kinds of music with all sorts of people. There's even a real choice of films at the movie theaters around town. And then, of course, there's the gay and lesbian scene, a whole subset of nightlife easily accessible to visitors. Still, the nightlife here is not as action-packed as the scene in New York or Los Angeles. Bars close at 2am.

If there's a center of nightlife in the city, it's **South of Market (SoMa)** with its mix of straight and gay places to drink, dance and listen to music. **The Mission** comes in second, with bars and theaters scattered along 16th and 17th Sts. There's a third entertainment zone from **Civic Center** to the Van Ness Ave multiplexes. Downtown, theaters from Union Square to Yerba Buena Center vie with the bars and clubs of **North Beach**.

Listings

For the best and latest information on who's doing what where, check the entertainment pages of the **SF Weekly** and the **Bay Guardian**, the free alternative papers available all over town. The **San Francisco Chronicle** coverage is good, though limited by its need to cover the entire Bay Area. The website **e www .sfstation.com** is another good source. For gay and lesbian entertainment, get the **BAR**, **Frontiers** or **Odyssey**, all distributed weekly in most of the neighborhoods in the center of the city.

Jam session at the Elite Cafe (p. 79)

Anthony Pidgeon

SPECIAL EVENTS

January *Independent Film Festival* – mid-January at the Lumiere on California St and the Fine Arts in Berkeley
Chinese New Year – the Golden Dragon Parade rolls through downtown late January or early February

March *St Patrick's Day* – March 17; Irish Americans and friends march down Market St and refresh themselves all around town

April *Cherry Blossom Festival* – late April; martial arts, dancing and other events in Japantown
International Film Festival – late April to early May; two weeks of films at venues all over the city

May *Cinco de Mayo* – weekend closest to May 5; festival and parade down Mission St celebrating victory of the Mexicans over the French
Bay to Breakers – third Sunday; 100,000 runners in every conceivable form of dress and undress do the 7 miles from the Embarcadero to Ocean Beach
Carnaval – Memorial Day weekend; Mardi Gras–style parade down Mission St

June *International Lesbian & Gay Film Festival* – last two weeks of the month at Castro Theater and other venues
Pride Parade – last Sunday; up to a half-million marchers and spectators celebrate gay pride

July *Independence Day* – July 4; fireworks on the bay offshore from Fisherman's Wharf and Aquatic Park

September *Opera in the Park* – first Sunday following the start of opera season; free show at Sharon Meadow in Golden Gate Park
San Francisco Blues Festival – mid- to late September; two days of blues on the Great Meadow at Fort Mason
Folsom St Fair – late September; tens of thousands of leather folk and average folk who like a show converge for a street fair with a difference

October *Castro St Fair* – first weekend; arts and crafts, music and food, masses of gays and lesbians
Jazz Festival – late October and early November; performances in venues all around town
Halloween – October 31; the entire city dresses up from morning to night; crowds converge on the Castro to gawk and on Civic Center to dance to live music

Free noontime concerts take place at Yerba Buena Gardens in summer.

BARS & PUBS

Buena Vista (4, A5)

This place gave Irish coffee to the world, and it's been living off that achievement ever since. Bartenders here serve over 2000 glasses of the stuff every day. Take a load off your feet and enjoy the view of the bay.
✉ 2765 Hyde St
☎ 474-5044
Ⓜ Powell-Hyde cable car ☐ 10, 19, 30, 47
🕐 Mon-Fri 9am-2am, Sat & Sun 8am-2am
♿ 21+ after 9:30pm

G-Bar (3, D6)

The bar du jour for Pacific Heights 30-somethings is in a 1960s motel that washed up on the corner of Presidio and California. The interior recalls LA restaurants of the '40s and '50s like Scandia. The customers are straight out of a J Crew or Polo catalog.
✉ 488 Presidio Ave
☎ 409-4227 ☐ 1, 3, 43 🕐 Mon-Sat 5:30pm-1:30am ♿ 21+

Gordon Biersch (5, H9)

This huge, noisy microbrewery set in a corner of the old Hills Bros coffee plant overlooks the Embarcadero and the Bay Bridge. The brews and burgers are the draw; the views are just a bonus.
✉ 2 Harrison St
☎ 243-8246 Ⓜ Muni F line ☐ 12 🕐 Sun-Tues 11:30am-11pm, Wed & Thurs 11:30am-midnight, Fri & Sat 11:30am-1am
♿ all ages

Harry's on Fillmore (4, E3)

There are bars for everyone and everything in San Francisco. Harry's on Fillmore is for preppy types, the kind you thought disappeared around the last Ice Age. Nice, comfortable surroundings, a DJ with good tunes and a bar menu with good food.
✉ 2020 Fillmore St
☎ 921-1000 ☐ 2, 3, 4, 22 🕐 3:30pm-midnight (dinner served 6pm-10pm) ♿ 21+

Liberties (6, E4)

There's a new Ireland they tell us, and Liberties is a new Irish bar. It's still pulling Guinness, still presenting live music like a traditional Irish place, but also serving food worth coming for even if (Heaven forbid) you don't drink.
✉ 998 Guerrero St
☎ 282-6789 Ⓜ Muni J line ☐ 26 🕐 10am-2am ♿ all ages

Lucky 13 (6, B2)

If you ever wondered where bike messengers go after dark, follow the Umleitung (Detour) sign into the Lucky 13. You'll find a pool table, some pinball machines and a bar with beers from Bud to Chimay. Scary at first sight, comfy at second.
✉ 2140 Market St
☎ 487-1313 Ⓜ Muni Church ☐ 22, 37 🕐 Mon-Thurs 4pm-2am, Fri-Sun 2pm-2am ♿ 21+

The Plough and the Stars (2, A8)

This is about as close to an Irish working-guy's pub as you'll find in the city. People with real brogues share a drink after work or after dinner or even in lieu of dinner. There's Irish music six nights a week, Irish dancing from time to time.
✉ 116 Clement St
☎ 751-1122 ☐ 2
🕐 Mon 2pm-2am, Tues-Thurs 4pm-2am, Fri & Sat noon-2am ♿ 21+

Skylark (6, C4)

On a grungy block of 16th St, a neon sign, shiny plastic curtains in the window and a mass of carefully but casually dressed 20-something smokers announce one of the hipper clubs in this district of hip. Though a DJ spins tunes, it's more bar than dance club.
✉ 3089 16th St
☎ 621-9294 Ⓜ 16th

On the Town Alone

No need to sit around your hotel room alone watching a movie on Lifetime. There are plenty of places to enjoy a meal alone – try the counters at **Betelnut** (2030 Union St; 4, C3), **Chow** (p. 71) or **Mario's** (p. 79) for starters – and single tickets to performances are often easier to find than tickets for two or three people (just show up early; there's usually someone with an extra ticket to sell). Tickets for singles are frequently easy to come by for concerts and theaters. For drinking and lounging, try **G-Bar** (above), **Tosca Cafe** (p. 87) or the **Hayes and Vine Wine Bar** (437 Hayes St; 4, G5; ☎ 626-5301).

St BART 🚌 14, 22, 26, 49 🕐 7pm-2am ♿ 21+

Toronado (6, A2)
This funky joint has 40 or 50 kinds of beer, on tap and in bottles, with lots of choices from the best breweries in Belgium and Germany. Buy a sausage from Rosamunde next door.
✉ 547 Haight St
☎ 863-2276 Ⓜ Muni Church 🚌 6, 7, 22, 66, 71 🕐 11:30am-2am (closed Christmas) ♿ 21+

Tosca Cafe (5, F5)
Tosca did not need a mink coat to become a legend. The old-world bar, the tall espresso machine and the opera on the jukebox set a nice stage, and the celebrities sprinkled in the crowd amid less-known regulars put on a little show.
✉ 242 Columbus Ave
☎ 391-1244 🚌 15, 41, 45 🕐 Tues-Sat 5pm-2am ♿ 21+

Anthony Pidgeon

The Beats go on at Vesuvio, 255 Columbus Ave.

COFFEEHOUSES

Atlas Cafe (3, F8)
At this neighborhood spot, slackers and still-employed dot-commies hang out over coffee or terrific (if simple) coffee-shop food. Live music Thursday night and Saturday afternoon provides two more reasons to come.
✉ 3049 20th St at Alabama St ☎ 648-1047 🚌 27 🕐 Mon-Fri 7am-10pm, Sat 8am-10pm, Sun 8am-8pm

Brainwash (5, M4)
There are other places to get an espresso or sandwich while you do your wash, but there aren't many that also have live perform-

ances. It's almost as cutting-edge as it was when it opened 20 years ago, and just as entertaining.
✉ 1122 Folsom St
☎ 431-9274 🚌 12, 19 🕐 Sun-Thurs 7:30am-11pm, Fri & Sat 7:30am-midnight

Cafe Flore (6, C2)
This coffeehouse consists of a greenhouse and a shed filled with the sound of music and the smell of great coffee-shop food from the kitchen. Busy from morning to night, it draws an eclectic crowd of gays, punks and visitors (some of whom may be gay and punk and visiting

all at once).
✉ 2298 Market St
☎ 621-8579 Ⓜ Muni Castro 🚌 24 🕐 7am-11pm

Cafe Roma (5, E4)
With a great location in North Beach just below Washington Square, Cafe Roma approaches the feel of an Italian cafe on warm days, when the place seems to spill out onto the sidewalk.
✉ 526 Columbus Ave
☎ 296-7942 🚌 15, 30, 41, 45 🕐 Mon-Thurs 6am-7pm, Fri 6am-8pm, Sat 7am-midnight, Sun 7am-8pm

Excellent people-watching at Cafe Flore, in the Castro

Caffe Trieste (5, E4)
Not as glamorous as Tosca but every bit as authentic, this survivor from the days of Ferlinghetti, Kerouac and Ginsberg still dispenses some of the best espresso in the city, along with pastries and sandwiches that fuel the body as the scene around you fuels the soul.

Pen your own poetry here.
✉ 601 Vallejo St
☎ 392-6739 🚌 15, 30, 41, 45 ⏰ Sun-Thurs 6:30am-11pm, Fri & Sat 6:30am-midnight

Farley's (3, F9)
Potrero Hill is like a small town on the edge of the city, and Farley's is a small-town hangout. A little funky for the Starbucks set, it serves coffee, espresso and delectable pastries and sells magazines and newspapers.
✉ 1315 18th St at Texas St ☎ 648-1545
🚌 22 ⏰ Mon-Fri 6:30am-10pm, Sat & Sun 8am-10pm

DANCE CLUBS

111 Minna (5, J6)
Every Friday night, this gallery on the edge of the Financial District hosts Stir-Fri-days, a free party hosted by DJs Jason Fluid and Maneesh the Twister (and whoever they get to join them). The mix of people and sounds here is very San Francisco.
✉ 111 Minna St
☎ 974-1719
Ⓜ Montgomery 🚌 5, 6, 7, 14, 21, 66, 71
⏰ Fri 5pm-9pm, check calendar for other events ♿ 21+

1015 Folsom St (5, M4) A coed bathhouse in the 1970s, 1015 now has two dance floors on three levels, two bars and sound strong enough to clean your clothes. It's usually straight, and always popular. Be prepared for a pat-down before you enter (there's a serious no-drugs policy after some problems with the SFPD).
✉ 1015 Folsom
☎ 431-1200 🅴 www .1015.com 🚌 12, 27
⏰ Thurs-Sun 10pm-

6am (hours may vary with events) ♿ 21+

The Endup (5, M5)
This South of Market institution illustrates San Francisco in all its polymorphous pansexuality. Very gay on Fag Fridays, very lesbian for Kandy Bar on Saturdays, very mixed other times. The Sunday T-dance begins early in the morning as parties wind down elsewhere, and roars into the afternoon.
✉ 995 Harrison St
☎ 896-1075
🅴 www.theendup.com

🚌 12, 27 ⏱ Thurs
10pm-4:30am, Fri
10pm-6am, Sat 6am-
4pm, 10pm-4am, Sun
6am-8pm ♿ 21+

Harry Denton's Starlight Room (5, H4)

This is the place to go
when you want to feel like
a glamorpuss from a black-
and-white movie.
Overlooking Union Square
high atop the Drake Hotel,
as they used to say on the
radio, it's dressy, pricey and
worth every bit of the time,
effort and money.
✉ 450 Powell St
☎ 395-8595 🄴 www
.harrydenton.com
Ⓜ Powell, Powell-Hyde
& Powell-Mason cable
cars 🚌 2, 3, 4, 38
⏱ 4:30pm-2am ♿ 21+

Holy Cow (5, O2)

A fixture since the late
1980s, when SoMa turned
straight or at least not
exclusively gay, Holy Cow
has mainstream music with
a hint of an edge and an
easy atmosphere, which
may help account for the
lines late at night year
after year.
✉ 1535 Folsom St
☎ 621-6087 🚌 12, 27
⏱ Wed 9pm-2am,
Thurs-Sat 8pm-2am
♿ 21+

Justice League (4, H2)

It's home of Club Dread
every Monday, with reggae
and other sounds from the
islands. Hear DJs from
around town and around
the country and the occa-
sional live act, playing hip
hop and other urban
sounds.
✉ 628 Divisadero St
☎ 440-0409 🚌 24
⏱ schedule varies, gen-
erally 9pm-2am ♿ 21+

Metronome Ballroom (3, F9)

If you've had it with
disco, try real dancing,
from swing to salsa, at the
Metronome's parties Friday,
Saturday and Sunday
nights (with or without a
lesson, though lessons
might help).
✉ 1830 17th St
☎ 252-9000 🚌 9, 22
⏱ classes nightly,
dance party hours vary
♿ all ages

Ruby Skye (5, J3)

Where most San Francisco
clubs lean toward funky,
Ruby Skye leans toward
chic. Housed in the old
Stage Door movie palace,
RS sparks the scene with
fire-eaters and other circus
performers. Other attrac-
tions include a VIP room
for you-know-whos and a
smoking lounge.
✉ 420 Mason St
☎ 693-0777
🄴 www.rubyskye.com
Ⓜ Powell, Powell-Hyde
& Powell-Mason cable
cars 🚌 2, 3, 4, 38
⏱ Wed-Fri 9am-3am,
Sat 8am-3am ♿ 21+

Sound Factory (5, K8)

Three huge dance floors
feature different variations
of hip hop and house
music for a young, mainly
straight crowd. The Sound
Factory is open Saturday
night, with special events
and theme parties held
other nights.
✉ 525 Harrison St
☎ 546-7938 🚌 12,
10, 15 ⏱ Sat 9pm-4am
♿ 21+

Nighttime is the right time on Fillmore St.

CINEMAS

AMC 1000 (4, F5)
This 10-screen megaplex is tucked into a landmark building designed in the 1920s as an automobile dealership. It offers stadium seating, advance ticketing and the usual Hollywood releases.
✉ 1000 Van Ness Ave
☎ 922-4262 e www.amctheaters.com 🚍 2, 3, 4, 38, 47, 49

AMC Kabuki 8 (4, F3)
This really was a Kabuki theater. It's now an eight-screen multiplex (read: good concessions, good sound, no stadium seating) at the junction of Pacific Heights and Japantown, making it one of your best choices for dinner and a show.
✉ 1881 Post St
☎ 931-9800 e www.amctheaters.com
🚍 22, 38

Castro Theatre

Film Festivals
There's a film festival showing somewhere almost any time of the year. The biggies include the **San Francisco International Film Festival** from mid-April to May, the **International Lesbian & Gay Film Festival** in June, the **Jewish Film Festival** in late July and early August, and **Spike and Mike's Festival of Animation** twice a year, in April and November.

Castro Theatre (6, C1)
The Castro is a 1920s movie palace that was never cut up or cleaned up. It still has an organist to play before the main feature in the evening (he closes every performance with 'San Francisco'). Too big to call an 'art house,' but far too arty to be called a regular movie theater.
✉ 429 Castro St
☎ 621-6120 🚇 Muni Castro 🚍 24, 35, 37

Embarcadero Center Cinema (5, F6)
This five-screen theater is run by the Landmark people, who present an interesting mix of first-run Hollywood releases, smaller Hollywood movies and foreign films, some even with subtitles. The theaters are small but comfortable.
✉ 1 Embarcadero Center ☎ 352-0810
e www.landmarktheaters.com
🚇 Embarcadero
🚍 1, 41

The Metreon (5, K5)
This is the behemoth of 4th St. There are 18 screens, including an IMAX, almost enough to fill the five-story garage across the street on a rainy day. See a Hollywood flick, have a bite in the food court, then play with the gadgets at Sony Style and PlayStation on the ground floor.
✉ 101 4th St
☎ 369-6000
e www.metreon.com
🚇 Powell 🚍 14, 15, 30

Opera Plaza Cinemas (4, G5)
Another great Landmark theater shows art-house and foreign films. Two of the four theaters are as tiny as screening rooms.
✉ Opera Plaza, 601 Van Ness Ave ☎ 352-0810 e www.landmarktheaters.com
🚇 Muni Van Ness
🚍 5, 47, 49

Pacific Film Archive (7, B5)
The PFA runs one of the best film programs in the world, with short series on subjects such as Islamic Women Directors and ongoing series on the history of film. The organization also cohosts the International Film Festival from late April to May.
✉ 2575 Bancroft Way
☎ 510-641-1412
e www.bampfa.berkeley.edu/pfa
🚇 Downtown Berkeley BART 🚗 I-80 east over Bay Bridge to University Ave exit, right on University to Oxford, right on Oxford to Durant, left on

Durant to College Ave
🕐 box office Mon-Fri
11am-5pm, evenings 1
hr before screenings

Red Vic Movie House
(2, D9) This is a Haight-
Ashbury institution. Come
sit down on an old sofa or
a padded bench and enjoy
the night's cult classic with
almost all the comforts of
home (except perhaps
smoking).
✉ **1727 Haight St**
☎ **668-3994** e **www
.redvicmoviehouse.com**
Ⓜ **Muni N line** 🚌 **6, 7,
43, 66, 71**

The Roxie (6, C4)
An art house, one of a
dying breed, showing any-
thing from French classics
like *Shoot the Piano Player*
to almost-underground US
flicks like David Mamet's
Lakeboat. It's one of the
few places to see documen-
taries or flicks with subtitles.
✉ **3117 16th St**
☎ **863-1087** e **www
.roxie.com** Ⓜ **16th St
BART** 🚌 **22, 26, 49**

No blockbusters at the Roxie

THEATER & COMEDY

American Conservatory Theater (5, J3)
San Francisco's premier
theater company is based
at the Geary Theater. It's a
stage for classics, revivals
and new work by the likes
of Tom Stoppard. The the-
ater school here was a
training ground for Danny
Glover, Annette Bening and
Denzel Washington.
✉ **415 Geary St**
☎ **749-2228**
e **www.act-sfbay.org**
Ⓜ **Powell, Powell-Hyde
& Powell-Mason cable
cars** 🚌 **2, 3, 4, 38**

🕐 box office noon-
6pm or showtime
(whichever is later)

Bay Area Theatersports (4, A3)
BATS has tried to improve
the improv business by turning it into a team sport. Two
teams compete in a series
of scenes and challenges.
Three judges award points
and determine a winner. You
judge for yourself.
✉ **Building B, Fort
Mason Center**
☎ **474-8935** e **www
.improv.org** 🚌 **22, 30**
🕐 shows Thurs-Sun 8pm

Berkeley Repertory Theater (7, A4)
The other great theater
company in the area is a
little more edgy than its
sister at the Geary in
downtown San Francisco.
Yes, they'll do
Shakespeare, but they'll
also do work by Tony
Kushner or Culture Clash,
a Latino trio, on one of
their two stages.
✉ **2025 Addison St**
☎ **510-647-2949**
e **www.berkeleyrep
.org** Ⓜ **Downtown
Berkeley BART** 🕐 **box
office noon-7pm**

Ticket Agencies

TIX Bay Area in the Union Square Garage (☎ 433-7827, **e** www.theatrebayarea.org) sells half-price tickets to performances at local theaters on the day of the show. It also sells full-price tickets in advance. **BASS** (☎ 776-1999, **e** www.tickets.com) is the 800-pound gorilla of the ticket business, with outlets at Tower Records and other spots across the Bay Area. **Mr Ticket** (2065 Van Ness Ave, ☎ 292-7328) also sells tickets but charges more.

Curran Theater (5, J3)
The other house in the tiny theater district on Geary St is home to national touring companies of big plays and musicals, like the Best of Broadway series or the latest Andrew Lloyd Webber.
✉ 445 Geary St
☎ 551-2000
Ⓜ Powell, Powell-Hyde & Powell-Mason cable cars 🚌 2, 3, 4, 38

Lamplighters Musical Theater (5, K6)
The Lamplighters have presented Gilbert & Sullivan operettas to San Franciscans since 1952. They currently split their time between the Yerba Buena Center for the Arts downtown and the Ira & Lenore Gershwin Theater, which is near the University of San Francisco (2350 Turk Blvd; 3, E5).
✉ 701 Mission St
☎ 978-2787 **e** www.lamplighters.org
Ⓜ Montgomery 🚌 10, 15, 30, 45 ⏱ box office Tues-Sun 11am-6pm

Magic Theater (4, A3)
Sam Shepard put the Magic on the map when he was resident playwright here, before Jessica Lange and the movies. It's still the

kind of place a Sam Shepard would work, two tiny spaces seating about 160 people apiece, showing new work by both established and not-so-established writers.
✉ Building D, Fort Mason Center ☎ 441-8822 **e** www.magictheater.org 🚌 22, 30
⏱ box office Wed-Sun noon-5pm

New Conservatory Theater (4, H5)
The NCT presents new work by young playwrights and old standards (including concert performances of classic musicals) on three small stages near Davies Symphony Hall.
✉ 25 Van Ness Ave
☎ 861-8972 Ⓜ Muni Van Ness ⏱ box office Tues-Sat 1:30pm-7pm

The Punch Line (5, F6)
The top comedy club in the city, this is where Margaret Cho plays when she comes home and where the headliners from the national circuit stop. Intimate surroundings with good sightlines enhance the experience.
✉ 444 Battery St
☎ 397-7573 **e** www.punchlinecomedyclub.com Ⓜ Embarcadero

🚌 1, 10, 41 ⏱ box office 1pm-6pm ♿ 18+

San Francisco Mime Troupe (6, D3)
The ACT of the left, the Mime Troupe is the premier guerilla theater company of the city. Expect political musical theater, half Irving Berlin, half commedia dell'arte, served up for free in Dolores Park and other parks every summer since the 1960s.
✉ Dolores Park
☎ 285-1720 **e** www.sfmt.org Ⓜ Muni J line 🚌 33 ⏱ check schedule for times and locations ♿ all ages

Theater Artaud (3, F8)
Before there were dot-coms, Theater Artaud was the place to see performance artists or performances by artists like the Kronos Quartet. It's still one of the hottest tickets in town for patrons who like performers who push the edge.
✉ 450 Florida St
☎ 621-7797 **e** www.theaterartaud.org
🚌 12, 22, 27 ⏱ box office Tues-Sat 1pm-4pm

War Memorial Opera House

CLASSICAL MUSIC, OPERA & DANCE

Audium (4, E4)
Every Friday and Saturday night, composer Stan Shaff presents his theater of sound-sculptured space, an audio experience of moving through space as sounds emerge from 169 speakers.
✉ 1616 Bush St
☎ 771-1616 e www.audium.org 🚍 2, 3, 4, 47, 49 ⏰ Fri & Sat 8:30pm (box office at 8pm)

Cal Performances
(7, A5) The University of California hosts most of the national and international touring companies as part of its arts series at Zellerbach Hall. See Merce Cunningham or Mark Morris or the Alvin Ailey dance troupe in spectacular surroundings.
✉ Zellerbach Hall, Bancroft Way at Telegraph Ave, Berkeley
☎ 510-642-9988
e www.calperfs.berkeley.edu
Ⓜ Downtown Berkeley BART ⏰ box office Mon-Fri 10am-5:30pm, Sat & Sun 10am-2pm

Herbst Theater (4, G5)
The intimate (900-seat) Herbst hosts all kinds of cultural programs, including classical music concerts, dance performances and the acclaimed City Arts & Lectures series.
✉ 401 Van Ness Ave
☎ 392-4400
e www.cityarts.com
Ⓜ Civic Center or Muni Van Ness 🚍 5, 21, 47, 49 ⏰ box office open 1hr before performances start

San Francisco Ballet
(4, G5) One of the oldest ballet companies in the US, it presents its repertory season at the Opera House and the smaller Yerba Buena Center for the Arts during the winter and spring and performs *The Nutcracker* every December, as one would hope.
✉ War Memorial Opera House, 301 Van Ness Ave ☎ 865-2000
e www.sfballet.com
Ⓜ Civic Center or Muni Van Ness 🚍 5, 21, 47, 49 ⏰ box office Mon-Sat noon-6pm (to first intermission performance days)

San Francisco Opera
(4, G5) San Franciscans have loved opera since the gold rush. The San Francisco Opera Company presents traditional and new work like the 2001

Anthony Pidgeon

production of *A Streetcar Named Desire* at the Opera House June to January. Standing-room tickets go on sale two hours before performances.
✉ War Memorial Opera House, 301 Van Ness Ave ☎ 864-3330
e www.sfopera.com
Ⓜ Civic Center or Muni Van Ness 🚍 5, 21, 47, 49 ⏰ box office Mon-Sat 10am-6pm

San Francisco Symphony (4, G5)
The San Francisco Symphony, under the direction of Michael Tilson Thomas, presents old favorites and new music at the Davies Symphony Hall from September to May.
✉ 201 Van Ness Ave
☎ 864-6000 e www.sfsymphony.org
Ⓜ Civic Center or Muni Van Ness 🚍 5, 21, 47, 49 ⏰ box office Mon-Fri 10am-6pm, Sat noon-6pm

Stern Grove Freebies
Every summer Sunday since 1938, 100,000 San Franciscans have converged on the wooded canyon at the corner of 19th Ave and Sloat Blvd (3, H3) to enjoy the symphony, the opera, the ballet or pop music from the likes of Eddie Palmieri or Les Yeux Noir, all for free. For the season's schedule, go to e www.sterngrove.org, or call ☎ 252-6252.

JAZZ, BLUES & ROCK

Bill Graham Civic Auditorium (5, M2)
This 5000-seat auditorium fills that gap between a music hall and an arena. The Civic Auditorium has hosted everything from the San Francisco Opera to the Grateful Dead, who used to play here on New Year's Eve.
✉ 99 Grove St
☎ 974-4000 Ⓜ Civic Center 🚌 9, 19, 21, 26 ♿ all ages unless posted

Bimbo's 365 (5, D2)
This old-fashioned nightclub has adapted to the times over and over. Rita Hayworth danced in the chorus line here, but you'll be going to see The Faint, Pride & Joy or Super Furry Animals.
✉ 1025 Columbus Ave
☎ 474-0365 e www .bimbos365club.com 🚌 15, 30 ⏲ box office Mon-Fri 10am-4pm ♿ 21+ unless posted otherwise

Boom Boom Room (4, F3)
The Room has been booming with the sounds of rhythm & blues and the sights of drinking and dancing since the 1930s, through the hot times of the '40s and not-so-hot times of urban renewal and

Elvis Presley that followed.
✉ 1601 Fillmore St
☎ 673-8000 e www .boomboomblues.com 🚌 22, 38 ⏲ 4pm-2am, shows start 9pm ♿ 21+

Bottom of the Hill (3, F9)
This club is everything a neighborhood dive should be: comfy verging on funky. It hosts live music from good up-and-coming bands seven nights a week. There's food to eat, beer to drink and a patio where you can enjoy a smoke. No wonder *Rolling Stone* called it the best place for live music in town.
✉ 1233 17th St
☎ 621-4455 e www .bottomofthehill.com 🚌 19, 22 ⏲ Sun-Thurs 3pm-2am, Fri 2pm-2am, Sat 8:30pm-2am ♿ 21+ unless otherwise posted

Cafe du Nord (6, B2)
Anything goes at this club, from jazz singers like Ledisi to the Gun and Doll Show. Eric Shea's Monday Night Hoot is a musical variety show featuring eight to 10 acts that made this week's cut. Happy hour is daily to 7:30pm, dinner Thurs-Sat 6:30pm-10pm.
✉ 2170 Market St
☎ 861-5016 e www .cafedunord.com

Ⓜ Muni Castro 🚌 22, 37 ⏲ Sun-Tues 6pm-2am, Wed-Sat 4pm-2am ♿ 21+

Covered Wagon Saloon (5, L5)
This SoMa bar covers the continuum from disco to grunge. Slink in for a drink in the afternoon or slide in for live music, karaoke or a look at the chubby go-go dancers in the evening.
✉ 911 Folsom St
☎ 974-1585 e www .cwsaloon.com 🚌 12, 27 ⏲ Tues-Fri 4:30pm-2am, Sat 8pm-2am, Sun 5pm-2am ♿ 21+

The Fillmore (4, F3)
Since Bill Graham put on a benefit for the San Francisco Mime Troupe featuring Jefferson Airplane on February 4, 1966, the Fillmore has hosted all the names of acid rock and most of the other names of rock that followed.
✉ 1805 Geary Blvd
☎ 346-6000 e www .thefillmore.com 🚌 22, 38 ⏲ box office show nights 7:30pm-10pm, Sun 10am-4pm ♿ all ages

Great American Music Hall (5, K1)
Just about every kind of music and musician play at the Great American Music Hall. There's good seating, downstairs or in the balcony above, good food and drink, good sound and sightlines to complement the acts.
✉ 859 O'Farrell St
☎ 885-0750 e www .musichallsf.com 🚌 19, 38 ⏲ box office Sun-

Concerts
The really big shows are all out of town, either indoors at the **Oakland Coliseum** (I-880 at Hegenberger Rd; ☎ 510-569-2121) or outdoors at the **Shoreline Amphitheater**, down the Peninsula (off Hwy 101 in Mountain View; ☎ 650-967-3000), or the **Chronicle Pavilion**, east of the city in Concord (2200 Kirker Pass Rd; ☎ 925-363-5701).

The Boom Boom Room, rocking since the 1930s

Mon 10am-4pm, Tues-Sat noon-6pm (to 9pm show nights) ♿ all ages

Paradise Lounge
(5, O3) There's lots of choices in Paradise, with three stages on two floors presenting acts from rock on the ground floor to poetry readings in the Above Paradise lounge. Free pool 3pm-7pm rounds out the entertainment here.
✉ 308 11th St ☎ 861-6902 🚌 9, 12, 47
🕐 3pm-2am ♿ 21+

Pier 23 Cafe (5, D6)
If you see a bunch of Harleys in front, it's probably a group of boomers here for the jazz or the R&B, not Hells Angels.

There's live music evenings and weekends in a lovely setting on the water, along with free salsa lessons on Wednesday.
✉ Pier 23 ☎ 362-5125
e www.pier23cafe.com
Ⓜ Muni F line 🕐 show-times usually 5pm or 10pm ♿ 21+

Slim's (5, O3)
This brand-name club on the 11th St strip is partly owned by Boz Scaggs, who lives up the hill in Pacific Heights. Originally a blues club, it features singer-songwriters, rock acts and a smattering of soul and blues groups.
✉ 333 11th St
☎ 255-0333 e www.slims-sf.com 🚌 9, 12, 47 🕐 box office Mon-

Fri 10:30am-6pm
♿ all ages

The Warfield (5, L3)
This old vaudeville theater is managed by the Bill Graham organization, which presents big-name acts here that don't want to perform in something the size of the Oakland Coliseum. You get all the sounds of the present and the conveniences of the past, including a restaurant and bar.
✉ 982 Market St
☎ 775-7722 e www.thefillmore.com
Ⓜ Civic Center 🚌 5, 6, 7, 21, 66, 71 🕐 box office at the Fillmore Sun 10am-4pm, show nights 7:30pm-10pm
♿ all ages

GAY & LESBIAN SAN FRANCISCO

The Cafe (6, C1)
A mixed (gay and lesbian), youngish (mainly 20-something) crowd hangs out here. Two dance floors, a pool table and a tiny balcony overlooking the corner of Castro and Market provide all the entertainment one could ask for.
✉ 2367 Market St
☎ 861-3846 Ⓜ Muni Castro 🚌 24, 35, 37
🕐 Mon-Fri 2pm-2am, Sat & Sun noon-2am
♿ 21+

Detour (6, C1)
If you step in from the sidewalk on a Sunday afternoon you'll need a minute for your eyes to adjust before you see the black interior accented with chain-link fencing, and the men hanging around waiting to connect at one of the cruiser bars in the Castro.
✉ 2348 Market St
☎ 861-6053 Ⓜ Muni Castro 🚌 24, 35, 37
🕐 2pm-2am ♿ 21+

Warehouse Parties
The biggest gay dance parties are held in showrooms and warehouses South of Market and in the Bayview District near the Produce Market, or in special venues like the rotunda of City Hall during Pride Week. Check the listings in *Frontiers* or the *BAR*, or pick up a flyer from one of the kids on the corner at 18th and Castro Sts.

The Eagle Tavern (5, P3)
Formerly the center of leather life South of Market, the Eagle is still very popular on Sunday afternoons, when men in every shape, size and costume fill the patio for the afternoon beer bust. Leather accessories are on sale inside, and there's lots of parking for motorcycles outside.
✉ 398 12th St ☎ 626-0880 🚌 9, 12, 47
🕐 noon-2am ♿ 21+

El Rio (6, G4)
'Your dive' may be the most festive bar in the city on a Sunday afternoon, when live bands play salsa on the patio and a crowd of lesbians mixed with gay men and straights who like to dance take to the floor.
✉ 3158 Mission St
☎ 282-2325 Ⓜ 24th St BART 🚌 14, 26
🕐 Mon 3pm-midnight, Tues-Sun 3pm-2am
♿ 21+

Esta Noche (6, C4)
The soundtrack and conversation at this Mission bar, with its young Latino crowd, are generally in Spanish. Come for the striptease on Friday night or the action any night.
✉ 3079 16th St
☎ 861-5757 Ⓜ 16th St BART 🚌 14, 22, 26, 49 🕐 2pm-2am ♿ 21+

Lexington Club (6, D4)
The only full-time lesbian bar in the city (as opposed to mixed clubs like The Cafe and clubs with women's nights like the Endup), this one has all the amenities: a pool table for play, booths for courting and a jukebox for background music.
✉ 3464 19th St
☎ 863-2052 Ⓜ 16th St BART 🚌 14, 26, 49
🕐 3pm-2am ♿ 21+

Martuni's (3, E7)
This piano bar up the street from Zuni Cafe draws

Where the boys are: Market St in the Castro

Anthony Pidgeon

The San Francisco Community Center (p. 98)

crowds every night with a winning combination of big, strong drinks, lively conversation and the occasional sing-along with the piano player. There's a good mix of music, good mix of orientations (mainly gay, some straight), and good mix of ages.
✉ 4 Valencia St
☎ 241-0205 Ⓜ Muni Van Ness 🚌 26
🕐 4pm-2am ♣ 21+

Mecca (6, B3)
From the minute it opened, this bar and supper club has been one of the most chic

nightspots in town, where fashionistas of every persuasion come to drink, to dine and to see entertainment running from cool jazz to hot drag. Very elegant space. Sensational music.
✉ 2029 Market St
☎ 621-7000 ℮ www .sfmecca.com Ⓜ Muni Castro 🚌 22 🕐 Mon-Sat 5pm-2am, Sun 4pm-2am ♣ 21+

The Midnight Sun
(6, C1) Midnight Sun has morphed from a conventional cruise bar into a video cruise bar, which

takes a certain amount of the tension out of waiting around to hook up.
✉ 4067 18th St
☎ 861-4186 Ⓜ Muni Castro 🚌 24, 33
🕐 noon-2am ♣ 21+

N'Touch (4, D5)
Long before Castro, there was Polk St. The Polkstrasse is no longer the center of the bar scene, but the N'Touch is busy as ever, drawing a heavily Asian crowd with amateur strip contests on Tuesday, real strippers on Thursday and go-go boys Friday and Saturday nights.
✉ 1548 Polk St
☎ 441-8413
Ⓜ California cable car
🚌 1, 19, 47, 49
🕐 3pm-2am ♣ 21 +

Pilsner Inn (6, B2)
Play pool, watch the foot traffic on Church St or hang with the mainly 30-something guys on the patio in the back at this easy neighborhood bar. It's

Sleep Overs

If you're looking for a gay-friendly place to stay, try one of the gay & lesbian B&Bs in and around the Castro, including **24 Henry Guesthouse** (24 Henry St; 6, B2; ☎ 864-5685, 800-900-5686), **Archbishop's Mansion** (1000 Fulton St; 3, E6; ☎ 563-7872, 800-543-5820), the **Inn on Castro** (321 Castro St; 6, C1; ☎ 861-0321) and the **Parker House** (520 Church St; 6, C2; ☎ 621-3222, 888-520-7275).

very busy Thursday, Friday and Saturday nights.

✉ **225 Church St**
☎ 621-7058 Ⓜ Muni Church 🚌 22, 37
🕐 10am-2am ♿ 21+

Powerhouse (5, O3)
Hot, hot, hot. Whether it's underwear night, uniform night or just Thursday night, this place oozes sex. Stick to your Levi's and leathers if you want to blend in. There isn't a dress code, but that skirt-and-sweater thing won't get you any dates here.
✉ **1347 Folsom St**
☎ 552-8689 🚌 12
🕐 4pm-2am ♿ 21+

The Rawhide II (5, M4)
This real country-and-western bar has real country music and real western dancing ($2 two-stepping lessons in the early evening are available if you're a city slicker or need a refresher). Saddle on up and come on down.
✉ **280 7th St** ☎ 621-1197 Ⓜ Civic Center 🚌 12, 19 🕐 4pm-2am ♿ 21+

San Francisco Community Center
(6, A3) The new center for the gay and lesbian, bisexual and transgen-

dered community opened in early 2002, offering meeting rooms, services and a safe home base for GLBT residents and visitors alike. Check out the view from the 4th-floor deck.
✉ **1800 Market St**
☎ 865-5555 📧 www.sfgaycenter.org
Ⓜ Muni Van Ness
🚌 26 🕐 Mon-Thurs 8:30am-10pm, Fri 9:30am-10pm, Sat 9am-10pm, Sun 10am-6pm ♿ facilities for gay youth available

SF Badlands (6, C1)
The Land of Bad is the best bar in the Castro, whether you're interested in drinking, dancing or cruising. Happy hours in the afternoons and beer busts Saturday and Sunday make your dollars stretch longer.
✉ **4131 18th St**
☎ 626-9320 Ⓜ Muni

Girl Stuff
Though there's only one full-time lesbian lounge in the city, there are dyke nights other places, from Kandy Bar Saturday night at the **Endup** (p. 88), to Junk the last Sunday of the month at **Cafe du Nord** (p. 94), to different women's shows Friday night at **The Stud** (below).

Castro 🚌 24, 33
🕐 2am-2pm ♿ 21+

The Stud (5, O4)
Hip young guys have made The Stud their spot to drink and dance for almost 30 years, first on Folsom St at the present location of the Holy Cow, now deeper in the heart of SoMa. It's home to Trannyshack on Thursday (think about it; you'll get it).
✉ **399 9th St** ☎ 863-6623 🚌 12 🕐 5pm-2am ♿ 21+

Theater Rhinoceros
(6, B5) The only theater in the city dedicated to performances by, of and for the gay and lesbian community has two stages (one small, one smaller). Expect more substance, less flesh than other gay-oriented stage shows around.
✉ **2926 16th St**
☎ 861-5079 📧 www.therhino.org Ⓜ 16th St BART 🚌 14, 22, 49 🕐 box office Tues-Sun 1pm-6pm ♿ all ages

Wild Side West (6, H5)
This lesbian-owned and operated bar in the most lesbian zip code in the city draws lots of lesbians and other neighbors from one of the most diverse areas in San Francisco.
✉ **424 Cortland Ave**
☎ 647-3099 🚌 24
🕐 1pm-2am ♿ 21+

Anthony Pidgeon

SPECTATOR SPORTS

In sports, as in music and food, San Francisco proves it is first rate. You'll find every kind of spectator sport you would expect in a large North American city, played at high-to-championship levels.

Tickets to popular teams can be a challenge. Call the team box office or **Ticketmaster** (☎ 800-551-7328) in advance, or try the concierge at your hotel if you're prepared to pay a bit of a premium.

Football

The **San Francisco 49ers** are the most popular team in town, bar none. Though it's been awhile since the 49ers won a Super Bowl, it's still hard to get your hands on a ticket for a home game at 3Com Park, also known as Candlestick Park (☎ 656-4900, [e] www.sf49ers.com).

The **Oakland Raiders** play at the Oakland Coliseum after a couple of years in Los Angeles. The bad boys of pro football have a devoted fan corps (hard core, one could say), but tickets are usually available (call BASS, ☎ 478-2277).

College football is almost as popular as the pro variety, particularly the weekend before Thanksgiving, when the **Stanford Cardinal** meet the **Cal Bears** in the Big Game, which alternates between Palo Alto (odd years) and Berkeley (even years). For Stanford tickets, check [e] www.stanford.edu, ☎ 800-782-6367; for Cal, check [e] calbears.ocsn.com, ☎ 800-462-3272.

Baseball

The Bay Area is blessed with two major league baseball teams, famous for their 1989 face-off in the World Series that was delayed by the Loma Prieta earthquake. The National League **San Francisco Giants** play at

Sports fans, San Francisco style

Pacific Bell Park (see p. 27), which is almost always sold out. Try the Giants website (**e** www.giants.mlb.com) for unwanted tickets from season-ticket holders.

The American League **Oakland Athletics**, or just A's, play at the Oakland Coliseum (I-880 at 66th Ave; ☎ 510-762-2255; **e** oakland .athletics.mlb.com), less than 30 minutes on BART from most parts of San Francisco. It's generally warmer here than Pac Bell Park. With the competition from a strong Giants team and the new Giants ballpark, A's tickets are easy to come by.

Basketball

The **Golden State Warriors** play in the Oakland Arena, next to the Oakland Coliseum, throughout the normal NBA season of November to May. Tickets are available online (**e** www.nba.com/warriors) or through the Warriors box office at 1011 Broadway in Oakland (☎ 510-986-2200, 888-479-4667).

Pacific Bell Park sits right smack on the bay, facing the Bay Bridge and the East Bay.

Anthony Pidgeon

places to stay

Some 17 million visitors come to San Francisco every year. At last count, over 100 hotels with over 33,000 rooms are competing for their business.

Most of those hotels and the lion's share of those rooms are in convention and business hotels clumped downtown between the Financial District and the Moscone Center, or around Fisherman's Wharf. Almost all were built in the past 25 years and have the modern conveniences (and inconveniences) that business travelers have come to expect.

Smaller boutique hotels fill the streets north and west of Union Square. Most were built as hotels in the 1920s and '30s, and many are showing their age. A good number have been refurbished – San Francisco is home to the Kimpton and Joie de Vivre hotel groups, which specialize in remodeling older properties – and some have been gutted completely to bring them into the 21st century.

None of this comes cheap. The average room rate before September 11 was about $155, with some seasonal variations (lowest in January and February, highest

Room Rates

The price ranges in this chapter indicate the cost of a standard double room before the 14% city hotel tax.

Deluxe	over $300
Top End	$200-300
Mid-Range	$125-200
Budget	under $125

from mid-September to mid-November when business travel is at its peak). Rates do fall off on weekends, less so during the prime vacation time of July to August. You can book a room for many hotels through Topaz Hotel Services (☎ 800-677-1550, e www.hotelres.com).

Feel the love in the dining room of Rosie's and Sami Sunchild's Red Victorian (p. 106).

Anthony Pidgeon

DELUXE

Campton Place Hotel

(5, H4) Campton Place may be the most elegant hotel in the city. Small (110 rooms) and chic, this hotel has service the Swiss would envy and a restaurant that's been a local landmark from the week it opened.

✉ 340 Stockton St
☎ 781-5555 fax 955-5536 e www.campton place.com Ⓜ Powell

Campton Place Hotel

🚌 2, 3, 4, 30
✗ Campton Place Restaurant

Clift Hotel (5, J3)

This is a makeover with mixed results by the Ian Schrager team that brought the Royalton to New York and the Mondrian to Los Angeles. If you like the sleek, modern, don't-you-know-who-I-am sensibility, you'll do fine.

✉ 495 Geary St
☎ 775-4700, 800-652-5438 fax 441-4621
e www.clifthotel.com
Ⓜ Powell 🚌 38
✗ Asia de Cuba

Four Seasons (5, J5)

The new entry in the luxury sweepstakes is in a sleek glass tower overlooking Market St and the Yerba Buena Center. Expect all the facilities and services this chain offers, and views

you'll only find here.
✉ 757 Market St
☎ 633-3000, 800-332-3442 fax 633-3001
e www.fourseasons
.com Ⓜ Powell 🚌 6, 7, 21, 66, 71 ✗ Seasons Restaurant

Mandarin Oriental

(5, G6) Not for those with vertigo. Perched high above the Financial District (so high even the hallways between the two towers have views), this is the most romantic business-traveler's hotel in the country, with service to match the views.

✉ 222 Sansome St
☎ 276-9888, 866-411-4766 fax 433-0289
e www.mandarin oriental.com
Ⓜ Embarcadero or Montgomery, California cable car 🚌 10, 15
✗ Silks

TOP END

Hotel Griffon (5, G8)

A small (57-room) hotel on the Embarcadero across the street from Rincon Center, the Griffon was renovated first in the 1980s and again in the 1990s after the Embarcadero Fwy was pulled, which created bay views for half the rooms.

✉ 155 Steuart St
☎ 495-2100, 800-321-2201 fax 495-3522
e www.hotelgriffon .com Ⓜ Embarcadero 🚌 2, 7, 9, 14, 21, 66, 71 ✗ Red Herring

Hotel Monaco (5, J3)

The flagship of the Kimpton Group is lushly

decorated from the lobbies to the guestrooms, equipped with gadgets from fax machines to coffee machines to Web TV.
✉ 501 Geary St
☎ 292-1000, 800-214-4220 fax 292-0111
e www.monaco-sf .com Ⓜ Powell 🚌 38
✗ Grand Cafe

Hotel Triton (5, H5)

The Triton may be just too flashy for its own good. With décor in its 140 rooms ranging from hand-painted blue diamonds on the walls to Zen Dens with daybeds, it takes San Francisco whimsy to a new

level, offering both Internet access and tarot readings.
✉ 342 Grant Ave
☎ 394-0500, 800-433-6611 fax 394-0555
e www.hoteltriton .com Ⓜ Montgomery 🚌 2, 3, 4 ✗ Cafe de la Presse (p. 82)

Huntington Hotel

(5, H3) Actors and opera stars stay at this Nob Hill landmark from the 1920s, which has been maintained as carefully as a socialite's face. Glorious views from almost every room complement the exceptional service.
✉ 1075 California St
☎ 474-5400, 800-227-

The Chains

All the big US hotel chains have properties in San Francisco. In addition to the chain hotels listed in this chapter, you can find four **Holiday Inns** (☎ 800-445-8667), two **Hiltons** (☎ 800-445-8667), four **Hyatts** (☎ 800-233-1234), a **Westin** (☎ 800-228-3000), two **Sheratons** (☎ 800-325-3535) and four **Marriotts** (☎ 800-228-9290).

4683 fax 474-6227
ⓔ www.huntington hotel.com Ⓜ California cable car ⓐ 1 ✗ The Big 4

Nob Hill Lambourne
(5, H4) This 20-room boutique business-traveler's hotel on the flank of Nob Hill has computer ports, fax machines, even kitchenettes in some of the suites to fix yourself a snack while you're working on that presentation for the morning meeting.
✉ 725 Pine St ☎ 433-2287, 800-275-8466 fax 433-0975 ⓔ www .nobhilllambourne.com Ⓜ Powell-Hyde & Powell-Mason cable cars ✗ Cafe de la Presse (p. 82)

Pan Pacific Hotel
(5, J3) Atlanta architect John Portman made his name designing hotels built around grand atriums, such as the Atlanta Hyatt Regency and here in Embarcadero Center. The Pan Pacific is Portman through and through, a touch of 1980s elegance beautifully maintained.
✉ 500 Post St ☎ 771-8600, 800-553-6465 fax 398-0267 ⓔ www .panpac.com Ⓜ Powell, Powell-Hyde & Powell-Mason cable cars ⓐ 2, 3, 4 ✗ Pacific

The Prescott (5, J3)
This 1920s hotel was beautifully restored by the Kimpton Group in an English-men's-club style that's a little easier on the senses than some of its sister hotels in the neighborhood. It's best known as the home of the Postrio Restaurant.
✉ 545 Post St ☎ 563-0303, 800-283-7322 fax 563-6831 ⓔ www.kimptongroup .com Ⓜ Powell, Powell-Hyde & Powell-Mason cable cars ⓐ 2, 3, 4 ✗ Postrio

Radisson Miyako Hotel (4, F3)
East meets West at the Miyako in the Japan Center, from the deep soaking tubs in the regular rooms in the tower to the traditional Japanese rooms (complete with shoji screens and tatami mats) in the garden wing.
✉ 1625 Post St

☎ 922-3200, 800-333-3333 fax 921-0417 ⓔ www.radisson.com ⓐ 2, 3, 4 ✗ Dot Restaurant

Sir Francis Drake Hotel (5, H4)
Fun, fun, fun – from the doorman in a Beefeater costume to the over-the-top 1920s lobby to the Starlight Roof overlooking Union Square. Enjoy the ambience of the old wings of the Fairmont or the St Francis without the crowds of conventioneers.
✉ 450 Powell St ☎ 392-7755, 800-227-5480 fax 391-8719 ⓔ www.sirfrancisdrake .com Ⓜ Powell, Powell-Hyde & Powell-Mason cable cars ⓐ 2, 3, 4 ✗ Scala's Bistro

W Hotel (5, K6)
This is the prototype of the Starwood Hotel chain's up-market properties for the hip and the wannabe. It's a winning formula, with rooms that look like dressing rooms in a nice Banana Republic and a lobby filled with PIB (people in black) from morning to night.
✉ 181 3rd St ☎ 777-5300, 877-946-8357 fax 817-7823 ⓔ www.starwood.com Ⓜ Montgomery ⓐ 10, 15, 30, 45 ✗ XYZ

Bed & Breakfast
There are scores of B&Bs scattered around the city. **Bed & Breakfast San Francisco** (☎ 899-0600, fax 899-9923, ⓔ www.bbsf.com) represents about two dozen properties.

California B&B Travel Directory (ⓔ www .bbtravel.com) claims to list more than 1300 B&Bs statewide, including a large number in San Francisco.

MID-RANGE

Abigail Hotel (5, L2)
This small (60-room) European-style place is best known for the Millennium restaurant, with its high-style vegan cuisine. The location on the tough side of the Civic Center means good deals for visitors, even better for visitors looking for weekly or monthly rates.
✉ **246 McAllister St**
☎ **861-9728 fax 861-5848** e **www.abigail hotel.com** Ⓜ **Civic Center** 🚌 **5, 19**
✕ **Millennium**

Comfort Inn by the Bay (4, B4)
This otherwise graceless chain-style hotel has three things going for it: low prices, a nice location within walking distance of Ghirardelli Square and the shops and restaurants on Union St, and picture-postcard views of the bay and the Golden Gate Bridge from the north side.
✉ **2775 Van Ness Ave**
☎ **928-5000, 800-228-5150 fax 431-3990**
e **www.hotelchoice .com** 🚌 **49** ✕ **Pluto's (p. 80)**

Commodore Hotel (5, J2) This small Union Square–adjacent hotel was built in a vaguely art deco style in the 1920s and renovated in the 1990s to add cable TV, computer ports and other necessities of modern life. It's home of the Red Room bar, one of the spots of the moment.
✉ **825 Sutter St**
☎ **923-6800, 800-338-6848 fax 923-6804**
e **www.thecommodore hotel.com** 🚌 **2, 3, 4**
✕ **Titanic Cafe**

Dolores Park Inn (6, C3) Each room is individually decorated with antiques and queen-size beds in this Victorian mansion converted into an elegant hideaway. Don't concern yourself over which celebrities have stayed here, just be a celebrity in your own right. A two-night minimum applies.
✉ **3641 17th St** ☎ **621-0482 fax 621-0482**
Ⓜ **Muni J line** 🚌 **22, 33** ✕ **Dolores Park Cafe (501 Dolores St)**

Hotel Beresford Arms (5, J2) The Beresford Arms and its sister hotel, the Beresford (635 Sutter St, ☎ 673-9900), are good examples of the small older hotels to be found along Post and Sutter Sts west of Union Square. The rooms are well maintained, the service gracious if slapdash at times.
✉ **701 Post St**
☎ **673-2600, 800-533-6533 fax 929-1535**
e **www.beresford.com**
🚌 **2, 3, 4, 38** ✕ **Dottie's True-Blue Cafe (522 Jones St)**

Hotel Boheme (5, E4)
This zippy place in North Beach was recently renovated to recapture the feel of North Beach in the 1950s while adding the conveniences of the 1990s (we're talking Kerouac with comfort).
✉ **444 Columbus Ave**
☎ **433-9111 fax 362-6292** e **www.hotel boheme.com** 🚌 **30, 15, 41, 45** ✕ **Mario's Bohemian Cigar Stand Café (p. 79)**

Hotel Rex (5, H4)
When you want elegance and don't want to pay for the Campton Place, come stay at the 96-room Hotel Rex, in the middle of the prime Union Square shopping area and completely dolled up with writing desks, CD players and dataports for travelers on the go.
✉ **562 Sutter St**
☎ **433-4434, 800-433-4434 fax 433-3695**
e **www.sftrips.com**
Ⓜ **Powell, Powell-Hyde & Powell-Mason cable cars** 🚌 **2, 3, 4**
✕ **Vicious Circle Lobby Lounge**

Majestic Hotel (4, E4)
San Francisco's oldest continually operated hotel was built as a private residence at the turn of the last century, was converted to a hotel in 1904 and survived the earthquake and fire of 1906. Its guestrooms retain the sensibility of that time, with modern conveniences for guests of this time – the best of both worlds.
✉ **1500 Sutter St**
☎ **441-1100, 800-869-8966 fax 673-7331**
e **www.thehotel majestic.com** 🚌 **2, 3, 4**
✕ **Perlot**

Queen Anne Hotel (4, E4) A romantic option, this Victorian from the 1890s has 48 rooms, some with wood-burning fireplaces, all with private baths and extras like breakfast in the morning and car service to downtown. Its location makes it convenient to Pacific Heights and Japantown destinations.

✉ **2220 Sacramento St**
☎ **441-2828, 800-227-3970 fax 775-5212**
e **www.queenanne.com** 🚌 **2, 3, 4**
✕ **Florio (1915 Fillmore St)**

York Hotel (5, J2)
The York is another small Union Square–adjacent hotel, nicely updated to meet changing tastes. Best known as home of one of the better cabarets in town and as a back-ground in *Vertigo*.

✉ **940 Sutter St**
☎ **885-6800, 800-808-9675 fax 885-6990**
e **www.yorkhotel.com**
🚌 **2, 3, 4** ✕ **Dottie's True-Blue Cafe (522 Jones St)**

BUDGET

Andrews Hotel (5, J3)
Just two blocks west of Union Square, this hotel has small but comfortable rooms. The services are equivalent to hotels that are much, much bigger.

✉ **624 Post St** ☎ **563-6877, 800-926-3739 fax 928-6919** Ⓜ **Powell, Powell-Hyde & Powell-Mason cable cars** 🚌 **2, 3, 4, 38** ✕ **Fino Bar & Restaurant**

Beck's Motor Lodge (6, B2) This 1950s motel in the middle of the Castro is booked well in advance for big weekends like Pride, Halloween and the Folsom St Fair. Its charmlessness verges on charming. Its convenient location is simply unbeatable.

✉ **2222 Market St**
☎ **621-8212, 800-227-4360 fax 241-0435**
Ⓜ **Muni Castro**
🚌 **24, 37** ✕ **Cafe Flore (p. 87)**

Globe Hostel (5, N4)
There's no curfew at this quiet, friendly hostel in the middle of SoMa. Guests must show proof of travel plans to stay (no overnights for clubbers from the suburbs, though exceptions are made). Dorm rooms have five to seven beds each, and each has an attached bath.

✉ **10 Hallam St**

☎ **431-0540 fax 431-3286** 🚌 **12, 14**
✕ **Julie's Supper Club (1123 Folsom St)**

Hostel at Union Square (5, J4)
Location, location, location. One block off Union Square, a half-block from the Geary St theaters, this hostel has 285 beds in a combination of dorm rooms and private rooms. Reservations are accepted, so book ahead.

✉ **312 Mason St**
☎ **788-5604 fax 788-**

3028 **e** **www.norcal hostels.org** Ⓜ **Powell, Powell-Hyde & Powell-Mason cable cars** 🚌 **5, 21, 38** ✕ **Max's on the Square (398 Geary St)**

Hostelling International San Francisco City Center (5, K2) The HI people have converted a historic hotel into a plush new hostel, with 75 rooms in two-bed, four-bed and five-bed configurations, each with a private bath. Kitchen privileges, Internet kiosks and

Drive-In Motels

If you're passing through the city on a road trip and have to deal with a car, you may want to consider one of the old-fashioned motels that line Lombard St from Van Ness Ave to the Presidio, or one of the newer (okay, 1960s and 1970s) motels you'll find along Harrison and 7th Sts South of Market or on the side streets around Fisherman's Wharf.

Anthony Pidgeon

The Phoenix, '50s kitsch and home of the Backflip bar

Anthony Pidgeon

storage facilities make this a sensational base camp for an assault on the city.
✉ 685 Ellis St
☎ 474-5721, 800-909-4776 x62 fax 776-0775
ⓔ www.norcalhostels.org Ⓜ Powell, Powell-Hyde & Powell-Mason cable cars 🚌 19, 31 🍴 Mel's (1050 Van Ness Ave)

Phoenix Hotel (5, K2)
A study in contrasts: This 1950s motel complete with swimming pool and sun deck is a surprise in the Dashiell Hammett landscape of hotels and apartment buildings. The hip crowd in the hotel and the Backflip Lounge is an ever-bigger surprise given the neighborhood.
✉ 601 Eddy St
☎ 776-1380, 800-248-9466 fax 885-3109
ⓔ www.sftrips.com
🚌 19, 31 🍴 Mel's (1050 Van Ness Ave)

Red Victorian Bed, Breakfast & Art (2, D9)
The full name of the place says it all. This B&B in the middle of the Haight offers meditative art and a temporary community along with your bed and breakfast. The summer of love lives on here.
✉ 1655 Haight St
☎ 864-1978 fax 863-

3293 ⓔ www.redvic.com Ⓜ Muni N line
🚌 6, 7, 43, 66, 71 🍴 Cha Cha Cha (p. 75)

San Francisco International Hostel (4, A4)
This converted barracks at Fort Mason has 150 beds in arrangements ranging from four-bed rooms to 24-bed dorms that still feel like barracks. Kitchen, dining room and public rooms are there to eat and lounge in. Limited free parking.
✉ Building 240, McDowell Ave, Fort Mason ☎ 771-7277 fax 771-1468 ⓔ www.norcalhostels.org
🚌 30 🍴 Cafe Franco

San Remo Hotel (5, C3)
If you don't mind sharing a bath, the San Remo Hotel may be the best value in town. It's clean, comfy and charming, on a block where North Beach slides down toward Fisherman's Wharf. Workaholics and news junkies beware – there are no phones and no TVs to break the calm.
✉ 2237 Mason St
☎ 776-8688, 800-352-7366 fax 776-2811
ⓔ www.sanremohotel.com Ⓜ Powell-Mason cable car 🚌 30 🍴 Malvina (1600 Stockton St)

Seal Rock Inn (2, B1)
Hunter S Thompson used to stay here so he could hear the seals at night. Hear them bark for yourself, without the aids Thompson has been known to employ. Big rooms, great views.
✉ 545 Point Lobos Ave
☎ 752-8000 fax 752-6034 ⓔ www.sealrockinn.com 🚌 38 🍴 Seal Rock Inn Restaurant

Summer of Love room in the Red Victorian

facts for the visitor

Anthony Pidgeon

Muni's historic streetcars ply the F line.

ARRIVAL & DEPARTURE

Air

Three major airports serve San Francisco: San Francisco International (SFO), about 15 miles south of downtown; Oakland International, about 15 miles east of downtown; and San Jose International, about 50 miles south of downtown. Both SFO and Oakland have good connections to the city by car or shuttle bus. There is a good rapid transit service to Oakland on BART. (SFO service will begin in late 2002.)

San Francisco International Airport

SFO (1, C2) is one of the busiest airports in the country, serving approximately 41 million passengers in 2001. The new international terminal handles flights from Asia, Europe and Latin America, while the north and south terminals handle domestic flights, from shuttles to LA (the San Francisco–Los Angeles corridor is the busiest air route in the world) to trans-continental flights to New York City or Washington, DC.

Left Luggage

Storage lockers are unavailable for the indefinite future.

Information

General Inquiries
☎ 650-876-2377

Flight Information

Air Canada	☎ 888-247-2262
America West	☎ 800-235-9292
American	☎ 800-433-7300
British Airways	☎ 800-426-0333
Continental	☎ 800-525-0280
Delta	☎ 800-221-1212
Japan	☎ 800-525-3663
Mexicana	☎ 800-531-7921
Northwest	☎ 800-225-2525
Singapore	☎ 800-742-3333
United	☎ 800-241-6522
Virgin Atlantic	☎ 800-862-8621

Parking Information
☎ 650-877-8227

Hotel Booking Service
The travel agency in the international terminal (☎ 650-877-0422) can provide hotel reservations in addition to other services.

Airport Access

The Bay Area Rapid Transit (BART) connection to the airport is scheduled to open in late 2002. In the meantime, San Mateo County Transit runs express buses to the Colma BART station for $1.10. Check the BART website (e www.bart.gov) for details and fares.

SuperShuttle runs vans to downtown hotels for $12.50 per person (not including tips for the driver). Flag down a blue van on the curb outside baggage claim. To book a pick-up for a trip to the airport, call ☎ 800-258-3826. The Airporter runs buses to downtown hotels for $10-14 per person (no tipping). Catch the buses on the curb outside baggage claim.

Taxis are available at the stands in front of each terminal. Fares to downtown locations run $25-38 for up to five passengers.

Oakland International Airport

Oakland (1, C3) is about 15 miles east of downtown San Francisco – as close as SFO except during rush hour on the Bay Bridge. Its two smallish terminals handled 11 million passengers in 2001, chiefly on shuttle flights (it's the Bay Area terminal for Southwest Airlines) and long-distance flights to Atlanta, Chicago, Dallas, New York City and Hawaii.

Left Luggage
Storage lockers have been removed for the indefinite future.

Information
General Inquiries
☎ 510-577-4000

Flight Information
Alaska	☎ 800-252-7522
Aloha	☎ 800-367-5250
JetBlue	☎ 800-538-2583
Southwest	☎ 800-435-9792

Parking Information
☎ 510-633-2572

Hotel Booking Service
There is no hotel booking service at Oakland International Airport.

Airport Access
The AirBart shuttle runs from the terminals to the Coliseum BART station every 15 minutes. The trip takes about 10 minutes and costs $2. Buy tickets inside the terminal buildings (inbound) or on the ground level of the BART station (outbound). BART trains run about every 15 minutes, more frequently during rush hours. The trip into downtown San Francisco takes about 25 minutes and costs $2.75.

Taxis are available at the taxi stands in front of the terminal buildings. Fares to downtown hotels will run about $55, not including bridge tolls ($2) and tips. A number of private shuttles operate between Oakland and San Francisco and other places in the Bay Area. Shuttles into the city range from $22 to $40. Call the Oakland Ground Transportation Hotline (☎ 888-435-9625) for details.

San Jose International
The Norman Y Mineta San Jose International Airport is the stepsister of Bay Area airports, about 50 miles south of downtown San Francisco, just a few miles north of downtown San Jose. It's very convenient if you are headed to the South Bay, and not so convenient if you are headed anywhere north of Palo Alto. Like Oakland International, it mainly serves shuttle flights up and down the West Coast and longer flights to elsewhere in the US and Mexico.

Left Luggage
There are no storage lockers at San Jose Airport.

Information
General Inquiries
☎ 408-501-7600

Parking Information
☎ 408-277-3145

Hotel Booking Service
San Jose International does not have a hotel booking service, but its website (ⓔ www.sjc.org) has a map and list of nearby hotels and motels.

Airport Access
There is no straightforward ground transportation between San Francisco and San Jose International besides taxis (about $75) and private cars.

CalTrain (the suburban commuter line from San Francisco to San Jose and points south) stops relatively nearby in Santa Clara and San Jose; you can make a connection in a cab. Contact CalTrain at ☎ 800-660-4287 or ⓔ www.transitinfo.org.

Bus
San Francisco and Oakland are hubs for bus travel. Greyhound (☎ 800-229-9424, 800-231-2222; ⓔ www.greyhound.com) provides nationwide service from its main station at the Transbay Terminal in downtown San Francisco (425 Mission St; 5, H7) and somewhat more limited service from its terminal at 2103 San Pablo Ave (7, H4) in downtown Oakland.

Train

Train service in this part of the country is sketchy, and likely to become sketchier as Amtrak subsidies from the federal government come under review in 2002. Currently, the Coast Starlight stops in Oakland on its run from Los Angeles to Seattle, and the California Zephyr ends its journey from Chicago at Emeryville (next door to Oakland). Call ☎ 800-872-7245 or check [e] www.amtrak.com.

Travel Documents

Passport

Canadians need proof of Canadian citizenship or a passport to enter the US. All other visitors must have a valid passport, which should be valid for at least six months longer than the visitor's intended stay in the US.

Visa

Travelers from Argentina, Austria, Australia, Belgium, Denmark, Finland, France, Germany, Iceland, Ireland, Italy, Japan, Liechtenstein, Luxembourg, the Netherlands, New Zealand, Norway, Portugal, Singapore, Slovenia, Spain, Sweden, Switzerland, the UK and Uruguay can enter the US for up to 90 days under the reciprocal visa-waiver program if they have a roundtrip ticket that is nonrefundable in the US, and have a passport valid for at least six months past their scheduled departure date.

For the updated list of countries included in this program, see the Immigration and Naturalization Service website ([e] www.ins.gov) or call ☎ 800-375-5283. All other travelers will need a visitor's visa. Visas can be obtained at most US consulate offices overseas; however, it is generally easier to obtain a visa from an office in one's home country.

Return/Onward Ticket

Travelers under the reciprocal visa-waiver program will need return or onward tickets to enter the US. Travelers applying for visas overseas will generally require such tickets as proof of their intent to return home.

Customs

All incoming travelers must fill out customs declarations. Travelers must specifically disclose all agricultural products and all cash and cash equivalents worth $10,000 or more.

Duty Free

Overseas visitors may bring in up to $100 in goods or gifts duty-free, together with 100 cigars, 200 cigarettes and a liter of alcoholic beverages. As of this writing, Cuban tobacco products are still prohibited in the US.

Departure Tax

There are no separate departure taxes when leaving a US airport. Any airport charges are included in the cost of your ticket.

GETTING AROUND

San Francisco is one of the only places in California where you can get around without a car. There's a good public transportation system inside the city, and a reasonable network of planes, trains and ferries go out to the suburbs. You may need patience (the schedules can be sketchy off peak), and you may need some good shoes (a short walk can be a hike if it's straight uphill).

If you drive, you'll still need patience. Traffic is thick (there are more cars here per square mile than anywhere else in North America) and unpredictable (particularly around the bridges and tunnels). On-street parking is a challenge.

San Francisco is laid out in a set of grids mostly running north-south, laid over 43 steep hills that create the sensational views. Market St cuts a diagonal from the piers on the northeast waterfront to the foot of Twin Peaks at the center of the city.

Streets are numbered 100 to the block from beginning to end. Note that the numbered blocks don't always align (ie, the 100 block of one street might not be aligned with the 100 block of the next street over). To further complicate matters, the numbered streets start running southeast off Market St downtown, then turn a corner and begin to run east-west through the Mission and the Castro (so 3rd St crosses 16th St and so forth). Forty-eight avenues run coherently north-south across the Richmond and Sunset Districts from the east end of Golden Gate Park out to the beach.

Travel Passes

The San Francisco Municipal Railway (Muni; ☎ 673-6864) sells passports for one day for $6, three days for $10 and seven days for $15, good on all Muni conveyances other than express buses to 3Com Park. Buy them at the cable car turntable at Powell and Market Sts, at smoke shops and magazine stands around town or online at [e] www.sfmuni.org.

Fares throughout the Muni system are $1/35¢, free for children under four except on cable cars.

Buses take dollar bills, and there are change machines in the Metro stations. Some parts of the system are on the honor code, so hang onto the ticket you get when you enter. Those tickets are good anywhere on the system for two hours, except for cable cars, so transfers are easy.

Subway

The Muni Metro runs out Market St to the western and southern reaches of the city. It's a subway under Market St and Twin Peaks, a streetcar with limited stops out beyond. All five lines run from Embarcadero to Church St. Three of the five (K, L, M) run to Castro and West Portal. The other two lines (J, N) emerge from the subway at Church, three blocks short of Castro. The N is the only line that runs down the Embarcadero to Pac Bell Park and the CalTrain station. Trains run every five to 10 minutes during the day, every minute or so during peak hours.

Streetcars & Bus Lines

Muni buses serve the entire city all day every day. There is good service on most lines during the day, limited service in the evenings and 'Owl Service' on the main lines every 30 minutes from 1 to 5am. The historic F line streetcars run from Market and Castro Sts to the waterfront, then north along the waterfront to Fisherman's Wharf (see p. 18).

Train

The Bay Area Rapid Transit (BART) trains serve downtown and the Mission District as well as the East Bay and some suburbs on the San Francisco Peninsula near the airport. Service is fast and dependable. Fares vary based on the length of the trip.

A trip from downtown to the Mission District costs $1.10, while a trip from downtown to Berkeley runs $2.65. Call ☎ 989-2278 or check [e] www.bart.gov for details.

CalTrain provides commuter service from 4th and Townsend Sts in the South of Market area to the Peninsula, San Jose and Gilroy. Fares vary based on the length of the trip. A one-way fare from San Francisco to Palo Alto is $3.25.

Taxi

Taxis are usually easy to find in the center of the city and tourist zones like Fisherman's Wharf or the Castro. You can hail a taxi on the street, queue up at taxi stands in front of some major hotels, or call for a cab from one of the major companies such as De Soto (☎ 970-1300), Veterans (☎ 552-3181) or Yellow (☎ 544-1212). Taxis are harder to come by in the evening and near impossible on big nights like Halloween and New Year's Eve. Basic charges for rides inside the city start at $2.50, with 40¢ for each additional sixth-mile. (Those sixth-miles pile up quickly.)

Car & Motorcycle

Driving in San Francisco is difficult but not impossible. If you have a car, your biggest problem will be finding parking at your destination. There are large city garages open 24 hours a day at Sutter and Stockton Sts, 5th and Mission Sts, and under Union Square, Portsmouth Square and the Civic Center Plaza. Rates at Sutter/Stockton and 5th/Mission start at $2 for the first hour, going to $3 for two hours, $4 and $5 respectively for three hours, and $6 and $7 for four hours. Parking lots are few and far between outside downtown, and on-street parking in most neighborhoods is limited to two hours unless you have a neighborhood parking sticker. If you do park on any street that even resembles a hill, be sure to curb your wheels to keep your car from running away – it happens. (Turn the steering wheel away from the curb uphill and toward the curb downhill.)

Road Rules

San Franciscans drive on the right side of the road. As elsewhere in the US outside New York City, you can turn right on a red light after a full stop unless a sign says not to. Seat belts are compulsory for all front-seat passengers. Children under three must be strapped in safety seats.

The basic speed limit in the city is 30mph on the city streets. Driving under the influence of alcohol or drugs is strictly prohibited. (California has a 0.08% blood-alcohol limit, so you've been warned.) Designate a driver – you don't want to see the Hall of Justice from the inside.

Rental

You can rent from any of the big national car rental chains – Alamo, Avis, Budget, Hertz, Enterprise, National, Thrifty – at the airports and different spots in the city. Call national toll-free directory assistance (☎ 800-555-1212) for their telephone numbers. You will need a valid driver's license and a recognized credit card. Keep in mind that no one rents to drivers under 21, and many companies refuse to rent to drivers under 25.

Driver's License & Permit

Canadian and Mexican driving licenses are generally accepted in the San Francisco area. Other overseas travelers should carry their domestic driver's license and an international driving permit.

Motoring Organizations

The American Automobile Association (AAA), the preeminent motoring organization in the US, provides minor breakdown service, short-distance towing and other acts of mercy for its millions of members. Call ☎ 800-222-4357 for road service. AAA members can also get road maps at AAA offices and discounts from hotels and car rental companies. Call ☎ 800-922-8228, check e www.aaa.com, or go to the Civic Center office at 150 Van Ness Ave (☎ 565-2141, 800-222-4357).

PRACTICAL INFORMATION

Climate & When to Go

Summer is the busiest time in San Francisco, though it's true that a summer in San Francisco can be one of the coldest winters you'll ever experience. Expect fog and wind whipping down the streets at 30mph and long lines to board the cable cars. Wear layers you can take on and off as you move between the dramatically different microclimates around town.

The best times to visit San Francisco are in the spring after the winter rains have ended, and in the fall when the city enjoys long stretches of warm, dry weather. The winter rainy season can be wet and gloomy, but temperatures never go below freezing in town.

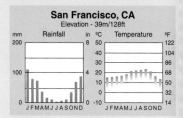

reservations to city guides and a free email newsletter you can download from its website. Log on at e www.sfvisitor.org, call at ☎ 283-0177, or visit at Hallidie Plaza (corner of Powell and Market Sts) Monday to Friday 9am to 5pm, Saturday, Sunday and holidays to 3pm (closed Easter Sunday, Thanksgiving, Christmas and New Year's Day).

Tourist Information

Tourist Information Abroad

The US has no tourist information offices overseas, so see the San Francisco–based services below or go to the helpful websites on p. 117 for information to help plan your trip.

Local Tourist Information

The San Francisco Visitors & Convention Bureau provides information, from maps and brochures about city sights and online hotel

Embassies & Consulates

Australia
   625 Market St, San Francisco CA 94104 (5, J5; ☎ 536-1970; after-hours emergency number for Australian nationals ☎ 888-239-3501)

Canada
   Canadian Government Trade Office, 555 Montgomery St, San Francisco CA 94104 (5, G5; ☎ 834-3180)

France
   540 Bush St, San Francisco CA 94108 (5, H4; ☎ 397-4330)

Germany
  1960 Jackson St, San Francisco CA 94109
  (4, D4; ☎ 353-0300)

Ireland
  44 Montgomery St, Suite 3830, San
  Francisco CA 94104 (5, H6; ☎ 392-4214)

Mexico
  870 Market St, San Francisco CA 94102
  (5, J5; ☎ 392-5554)

UK
  Citicorp Center, 1 Sansome St, Suite
  850, San Francisco CA 94104 (5, H6;
  ☎ 617-1300)

Money

Currency
US dollars are the only currency accepted in San Francisco. The US dollar is divided into 100 cents (¢). Coins come in denominations of 1¢ (a penny), 5¢ (nickels), 10¢ (dimes), 25¢ (quarters), 50¢ (half-dollars) and $1 (dollars). Although a new dollar coin has just been issued, one rarely sees dollar coins or half-dollar coins. Quarters are the handiest coins, for both vending machines and parking meters.

US bills are all the same color and the same size. They come in $1, $2, $5, $10, $20, $50 and $100 denominations ($2 bills are extremely rare).

Credit Cards
Major credit cards are accepted just about everywhere from hotels and restaurants to shops and gas stations. You will need major credit cards for certain transactions, such as renting a car, registering for a hotel room or buying tickets to a play or sporting event. Visa and MasterCard are the most commonly accepted, followed by American Express and Discover cards. Places that accept Visa and MasterCard usually accept Visa- or MasterCard-sponsored debit cards. Carry copies of your credit card numbers separately from your cards. If your cards are lost or stolen, contact the company immediately:

American Express   ☎ 800-528-4800
Diners Club   ☎ 800-234-6377
Discover   ☎ 800-347-2683
MasterCard   ☎ 800-826-2181
Visa   ☎ 800-336-8472

ATMs
ATMs are a good alternative to traveler's checks, particularly for overseas visitors who would otherwise have to stand in line somewhere to change money. They are all over town – in airports and train stations, outside banks and inside liquor stores. Almost all ATMs accept cards from the Cirrus, Star and Global Access networks. You'll be charged to use ATMs other than your own bank's (starting at 50¢). Most machines will disclose the amount of the charge and ask whether you want to proceed before they give you your cash.

Changing Money
Banks usually offer better rates than exchange offices. Most major banks change money during normal business hours. American Express has a local office at 455 Market St (5, H6; ☎ 536-2600; Mon-Fri 9am-5pm, Sat 10am-2pm). Thomas Cook has a downtown location at 75 Geary St (5, J5; ☎ 800-287-7362; Mon-Fri 9am-5pm, Sat 10am-4pm). Travelex has eight currency-exchange booths in the international terminal at San Francisco International. Hours vary based on flight schedules. Overseas visitors can also use their ATM cards to get US cash almost anywhere, at bank rates.

Tipping

Tipping is customary in bars, restaurants and better hotels. Tip your server at a restaurant 15% (unless the service is terrible) and 20% or more if the service is great. Tip the bartender $1 for one or two beers, 15% if you are buying a round. Tip taxi drivers $1 on a fare of $6 or less, 10% from there on up. Baggage carriers should get $1 a bag, and valet parkers $2 when they hand you the keys to your car. At your hotel, doorkeepers should get $1-2 to get you a taxi, the concierge $5 or more for booking a table or theater tickets, and the cleaner $1-2 a night.

Discounts

Many museums, tours and sights have discount tickets for children and seniors. If you are going to be in San Francisco for a few days, buy a CityPass at the visitors center (1 Hallidie Plaza, foot of Powell St) or from one of the participating venues. You'll save up to 50% on standard adult or children's admissions to five of the big attractions in town – the Museum of Modern Art, the Blue & Gold Fleet Bay Cruise, the Exploratorium, the Palace of the Legion of Honor and the Academy of Sciences/Steinhardt Aquarium. You also get a seven-day passport good on all Muni vehicles, including cable cars. You can purchase a CityPass in advance online at [e] www.citypass.net or by calling the SFVCB at ☎ 283-1077.

Student & Youth Cards

Most student and teacher discounts are reserved for students and teachers from local institutions.

Seniors' Cards

Seniors can get discounts at some sights and hotels. Ask if you don't see a sign. Some discounts apply to persons 50 and over, others to persons 60 or 65 and over. Seniors 65+ with a photo ID pay reduced fares on all Muni vehicles except cable cars.

Travel Insurance

A policy covering theft, loss, medical expenses and compensation for cancellation or delays in your travel arrangements is highly recommended. If items are lost or stolen, make sure you get a police report straight away – otherwise your insurer might not pay up.

Opening Hours

Most offices are open weekdays 8:30 or 9am to 5 or 5:30pm. Most shops are open seven days a week, from 10 or 11am to 6 or 7pm, noon to 6pm Sunday. Restaurants are usually open at least six days a week, from 11:30am to 2pm for lunch and about 5:30 to 10 or 11pm for dinner. Most shops are open on public holidays (except July 4, Thanksgiving, Christmas and New Year's Day), but banks, schools and offices are usually closed.

Public Holidays

Jan 1	New Year's Day
3rd Mon in Jan	Martin Luther King Jr Day
3rd Mon in Feb	President's Day
Mar/Apr	Easter Sunday
Last Mon in May	Memorial Day
July 4	Independence Day
1st Mon in Sept	Labor Day
2nd Mon in Oct	Columbus Day
Nov 11	Veterans' Day
4th Thurs in Nov	Thanksgiving
Dec 25	Christmas

Time

San Francisco is in the Pacific Standard Time zone, which is eight hours behind GMT/UTC. Daylight-saving time runs from the first Sunday of April to the last Saturday of October. At noon in San Francisco it's:

noon in Los Angeles
3pm in New York
8pm in London
6am (following day) in Auckland
4am (following day) in Sydney

Electricity

Electricity in the US is 110v and 60Hz. Plugs have either two or three pins (two flat, with an optional round grounding pin). Adaptors for European and South American plugs are available. Australians should bring adaptors.

Weights & Measures

Americans still use what they call the English system of weights and measures. Distances come in inches, feet, yards and miles; dry weights in ounces, pounds and tons; liquid volumes in pints, quarts and gallons. The US gallon contains about 20% less than the imperial gallon because it only amounts to 4 quarts. See the conversion table on p. 122.

Post

The Sutter Station in the Hallidie Bldg (150 Sutter St; 5, H5) and the Macy's Union Square Station inside the Macy's store (170 O'Farrell St; 5, J4) are the most convenient post offices or visitors. Other branches are listed under Government Listings in the phone directory white pages, or call ☎ 800-275-8777.

Postal Rates

Stamps are available at post offices and some bank ATMs. At press time, 1st-class mail within the US is 37¢ for letters up to 1oz (23¢ each additional ounce) and 23¢ for postcards. International airmail to places other than Canada and Mexico is 80¢ for a half-ounce letter and 70¢ for a postcard. Half-ounce letters to Canada and Mexico cost 60¢.

Telephone

Public telephones are usually coin-operated, though some pay phones accept phone cards, and some accept credit cards. Phone booths are relatively common, despite the recent explosion in mobile phone service. Local calls generally cost 35¢. Calls to the suburbs cost more.

The area code for the city of San Francisco and Marin County to the north is ☎ 415. The East Bay suburbs of Oakland and Berkeley are in area code ☎ 510. San Francisco Airport and the suburbs to the south are in area code ☎ 650. If you dial a number outside the area you're calling from, be sure to dial 1 first.

Phone Cards

Prepaid phone cards are sold at many newsstands and pharmacies around town, but they can be a rip-off. The MCI/Worldcom cards sold in various denominations at Walgreens may be the best overall value.

Lonely Planet's eKno Communication Card, specifically aimed at travelers, provides competitive international calls (avoid using it for local calls), messaging services and free email. Log on to ⓔ www.ekno.lonelyplanet.com for information on joining and accessing the service.

If you are using a credit card to make local calls, use a major carrier such as AT&T (☎ 800-321-0288) or Sprint (☎ 800-877-4646).

Mobile Phones

The US uses a variety of mobile phone systems, only one of which is a GMS remotely compatible with systems used outside of North

America. Most North American travelers can use their phones in the San Francisco Bay Area, but they should check with their carriers about roaming charges before they start racking up the minutes.

Useful Numbers

Directory assistance	☎ 411
International directory assistance	☎ 412-555-1515
International operator	☎ 00
Reverse-charge (collect)	☎ 0
Operator-assisted calls	☎ 01 (+ the number; an operator then comes on)
Time	☎ 767-2676
Weather	☎ 831-656-1725

International Direct Dial Codes
Dial ☎ 011 followed by:

Australia	☎ 61
Canada	☎ 1
France	☎ 33
Germany	☎ 49
Japan	☎ 81
New Zealand	☎ 64
South Africa	☎ 27
UK	☎ 44

Electronic Resources

You can check your email at the public libraries, including the New Main Library in the Civic Center (5, M2), at one of the local Internet cafes or by buying computer time at a branch of Kinko's.

Internet Service Providers
America Online (AOL) is the 800-pound gorilla of ISPs in the US. The other two major ISPs in the US are Microsoft Network (MSN) and Earthlink/Mindspring. Access AOL at ☎ 228-0009 or 240-4265, MSN at ☎ 430-9604 or 240-4676, and Earthlink at ☎ 376-0023.

Internet Cafes
Head to Chat Cafe (498 Sanchez St; 6, C2; ☎ 626-4700; Sun-Thurs 7am-8pm, Fri-Sat 7am-9pm; 30 free minutes with food & beverage), Quetzal (1234 Polk St; 4, E5; ☎ 673-4181; Mon-Fri 6am-11pm, Sat-Sun 7am-11pm; 16¢/min or $9.95/hr) or cafe.com (970 Market St; 5, K4; ☎ 922-5322; 8am-10pm; $1.25/10mins or $7/hr).

Useful Sites
The Lonely Planet website (e www.lonelyplanet.com) offers a speedy link to many of San Francisco's websites. Others to try include

San Francisco Chronicle
    e www.sfgate.com

San Francisco Visitors & Convention Bureau
    e www.sfvisitor.org

CitySync
CitySync San Francisco, Lonely Planet's digital guide for Palm OS handheld devices, allows quick searching and sorting of many SF attractions, clubs, hotels and more – all on scrollable street maps. Purchase or demo the product at e www.citysync.com.

Doing Business

The Kinko's store downtown at 50 Fremont St (5, H7; ☎ 512-7766) has workstations, fax machines, copiers and Internet access 24-7. Other locations have those facilities but may close earlier. Most large hotels and some smaller ones have business centers with workstations, fax machines, copiers and Internet access.

Travelers looking for information about doing business in the area should contact the SF Chamber of Commerce (Russ Bldg, 235 Montgomery St, 12th Flr; 5, H5; ☎ 392-4250; e www.sfchamber.com).

Newspapers & Magazines

San Francisco has two daily newspapers: *the San Francisco Chronicle* and the afternoon *San Francisco Examiner*. The *Chronicle* has a mixed reputation, to put it charitably. It's strong on lifestyle coverage like food, fashion and entertainment but weak on local – let alone national or international – news. You'll find *the New York Times* on sale all over town if you need a hard-news fix.

San Francisco Magazine is a glossy monthly catering to the professional classes, filled with restaurant reviews and cultural news. The *Bay Guardian* and *SF Weekly* are free weeklies with strong entertainment coverage, available in news boxes around town. The *BAR* and *Frontiers* are free weeklies for the gay and lesbian community.

Radio

San Francisco boasts two National Public Radio stations: KQED at 88.5 FM (most successful NPR outlet in the country) and KALW at 91.7 FM. KQED FM is about news and information, while KALW also has strong world music and new music programming. For conventional news radio, try KCBS at 740 AM. Find oldies on KFRC at 99.7 FM, classical on KDFC at 102.1 FM, hard rock on KITS at 105.3 FM, soft rock on KARA at 105.7 FM, Mexican pop on KSOL at 98.9 FM, soft R&B on KBLS 103 FM and hip-hop on KMEL 106.1 FM.

TV

You'll find the usual US suspects on the small screen. Every national network or quasi-network has a local affiliate, including the Spanish-language network Univision, which is carried on channel 14. There are three PBS affiliates: KQED (channel 9), KTEH (channel 54) and KCSM (channel 60).

Photography & Video

For high-end equipment and film, head to Adolph Gasser downtown (181 2nd St; 5, J6; ☎ 495-3852). For simpler stuff, try Brooks Camera downtown (125 Kearny St; 5, H5; ☎ 362-4702) or one of the many branches of Wolf Camera around town (2016 Market St; 6, B3; ☎ 626-4573). For processing, try Wolf, Ritz Camera (1 Hallidie Plaza; 5, K4; ☎ 835-3714) or almost any Walgreens drugstore. Overseas visitors shopping for videos must remember that the US uses the NTSC system, which is incompatible with the PAL (UK and Australasia) and SECAM formats (Western Europe).

Health

Immunizations
Neither vaccinations nor immunizations are required to enter the US.

Precautions
You can drink the water in San Francisco (it's fresh from the mountains), and you can breathe the air (the fog blows pollution away). If you do exercise or spend a lot of time walking up and down the hills, drink plenty of fluids and take breaks.

Like anywhere else, the usual precautions apply in San Francisco when it comes to sex. Condoms are available at any pharmacy and most corner stores. Use them.

Insurance & Medical Treatment
Overseas visitors should have medical insurance before they come to San Francisco, as medical care can

be very expensive in the US and many doctors and hospitals insist on payment before treatment.

Medical Services

The University of California, San Francisco Medical Center in the Inner Sunset (505 Parnassus Ave; 3, F5; ☎ 476-1000) is one of the great American hospitals, with all that entails. San Francisco General Hospital (1001 Potrero Ave; 3, G8; ☎ 206-8000) may look a little scary, but it has one of the best trauma units going.

Other hospitals with 24-hour emergency rooms include Davies Medical Center (Castro and Duboce Sts; 6, B1; ☎ 565-6060) and St Francis Memorial Hospital (900 Hyde St; 5, H2; ☎ 353-6300).

Pharmacies

The Walgreens pharmacies at 498 Castro St (6, C1; ☎ 861-6276) and 3201 Divisadero St (4, C1; ☎ 931-6415) are open 24 hours. There are other Walgreens on almost every corner, along with a dozen or so Rite Aid stores, including one downtown at 776 Market St (5, K3; ☎ 397-0837).

Toilets

You'll find some public facilities in the parks and about 20 big, green toilet stalls imported from France scattered around the city streets. The stalls cost 25¢ and are usually in good repair. You'll also find restrooms in the big hotels and shopping complexes and in the omnipresent Starbucks.

Safety Concerns

San Francisco isn't always the cool, gray city of love. Neighborhoods can change from gracious to dangerous in a block or two, so watch where you're going and use com-mon sense. Don't carry around huge amounts of cash, and lock up what you don't need if your hotel has a safe or safety deposit boxes. Don't carry your wallet in your backpack or your back pocket. Stay out of dim, empty streets after dark.

The main visitor areas from downtown to the northern water-front, around Pacific Heights, Valencia St and the Castro are very safe during the day and also quite safe at night if you stick to the main streets. The two areas to watch in particular are the Tenderloin (between downtown and Civic Center, roughly from Taylor to Hyde or Larkin) and Mission St from 15th to 17th or 18th Sts, which can be rough during the day and rougher at night.

Lost Property

The Muni lost & found department is located at 2620 Geary Blvd (4, F1; ☎ 923-6168).

Keeping Copies

Make photocopies of all your important documents; keep some with you, separate from the origi-nals, and leave a copy at home. You can also store details of docu-ments in Lonely Planet's free online Travel Vault, password-pro-tected and accessible worldwide. See [e] www.ekno.lonelyplanet.com.

Emergency Numbers

Police, fire, ambulance	☎ 911
Police information	☎ 553-0123
Rape crisis line	☎ 821-3222

Women Travelers

Women are as safe in San Francisco as they are in most any big US city. The usual precautions apply about paying attention to your surround-ings and taking a little extra care walking at night. Women may encounter obnoxious behavior after dark, particularly on the weekends, but most men will let it go if you just ignore them and keep on moving.

Tampons and pads are widely available, though there's a smaller selection of tampons than in Europe and Australia. The contraceptive pill is available by prescription only. Women from overseas who need refills of prescriptions should contact Planned Parenthood (☎ 800-967-7526). In case of emergencies, the 'morning after' pill is now available from Planned Parenthood without a prescription.

Gay & Lesbian Travelers

Not everyone in San Francisco is gay, but like gentiles in New York City, the straight San Franciscan majority lives in a world marked by the enormous number of gays and lesbians around them. Gays and lesbians are visible in every walk of local life, and simple gestures like hugs and handholding are as commonplace downtown as they are in the Castro. Gay-bashing and name-calling are rare but not unheard of. Like everyone else in town, gay and lesbian visitors should watch where they walk at night.

The Castro is the heart of the community, a place to meet or hang out on a sunny afternoon or to congregate in times of emergency. South of Market is clubland, home to most of the leather bars, half the dance clubs and half the sex clubs in town. Polk St still has a strip of bars and clubs, but it's a shadow of its 1970s self.

Information & Organizations
San Francisco has three gay weeklies – the *BAR* and *Frontiers,* which focus on community arts and politics, and *Odyssey,* which focuses on

community play. All are available free at newsstands and bookstores around town. The new Community Center at the corner of Market and Octavia Sts hosts dozens of organizations. Call them at ☎ 865-5555 for information.

For HIV-related questions, call the AIDS Nightline evenings at ☎ 434-2437. For other health questions, try the Lyon-Martin Women's Health Services at 1748 Market St (4, H5; ☎ 565-7667) or the Gay & Lesbian Medical Association (☎ 255-4547), which offers information and referrals weekdays from 9am to 5:30pm.

Senior Travelers

San Francisco is a popular destination for seniors. The public transit network and mild weather take the sting out of negotiating the hills, and the wide range of things to do – from museums to parks to night spots – appeal to travelers with almost any interest.

Information & Organizations
The San Francisco Commission on the Aging runs a gold-card program with city businesses that give discounts to seniors. Call them (☎ 800-510-2020) or visit one of the senior centers around town. The downtown/Tenderloin center is at 481 O'Farrell St (5, J3; open Mon-Fri 8:30am-5pm). The American Association of Retired Persons (AARP), a lobbying group for Americans 50 years and older, has hotel and car rental discounts for members. Call them at ☎ 800-424-3410, or log on at e www.aaar.org.

Disabled Travelers

San Francisco is a surprisingly good destination for the mobility impaired. All the Muni trains and many of the Muni buses are wheelchair accessible. Most of the major sights and most major hotels and restaurants are also wheelchair accessible. There are wheelchair cuts at the corners of most city streets, including blocks so steep the sidewalks have steps cut into the concrete.

Information & Organizations

The Independent Living Center of San Francisco (70 10th St; 5, N2; ☎ 863-0581) is a good general resource. Muni has its own accessible-services program. Call them at ☎ 923-6142. Mobility International USA (PO Box 10767, Eugene, OR 97440; ☎ 541-343-1284, fax 541-343-6812) advises disabled travelers on mobility issues and runs education programs. The Society for the Advancement of Travelers with Handicaps (347 Fifth Ave, Suite 610, New York 10016;

☎ 212-447-7284; e www.sath.org) publishes *Open World*, a magazine for disabled travelers.

Language

They speak American English in San Francisco, in a variety of accents ranging from California surfer dude to Hong Kong Chinese. Given all these different backgrounds, it's no surprise that the local lingo is largely limited to place names such as

The City – San Francisco

The Avenues – the Richmond and Sunset Districts in the west of the city

The Valley – depending on context, Napa or Central or Silicon

The Embarcadero – the waterfront, here or in Oakland

The 1000 block of Lombard, the 'world's crookedest street'

Conversion Table

Clothing Sizes
Measurements approximate only; try before you buy.

Women's Clothing

Aust/NZ	8	10	12	14	16	18
Europe	36	38	40	42	44	46
Japan	5	7	9	11	13	15
UK	8	10	12	14	16	18
USA	6	8	10	12	14	16

Women's Shoes

Aust/NZ	5	6	7	8	9	10
Europe	35	36	37	38	39	40
France only	35	36	38	39	40	42
Japan	22	23	24	25	26	27
UK	3fi	4fi	5fi	6fi	7fi	8fi
USA	5	6	7	8	9	10

Men's Clothing

Aust/NZ	92	96	100	104	108	112
Europe	46	48	50	52	54	56
Japan	S		M	M		L
UK	35	36	37	38	39	40
USA	35	36	37	38	39	40

Men's Shirts (Collar Sizes)

Aust/NZ	38	39	40	41	42	43
Europe	38	39	40	41	42	43
Japan	38	39	40	41	42	43
UK	15	15fi	16	16fi	17	17fi
USA	15	15fi	16	16fi	17	17fi

Men's Shoes

Aust/NZ	7	8	9	10	11	12
Europe	41	42	43	44fi	46	47
Japan	26	27	27.5	28	29	30
UK	7	8	9	10	11	12
USA	7fi	8fi	9fi	10fi	11fi	12fi

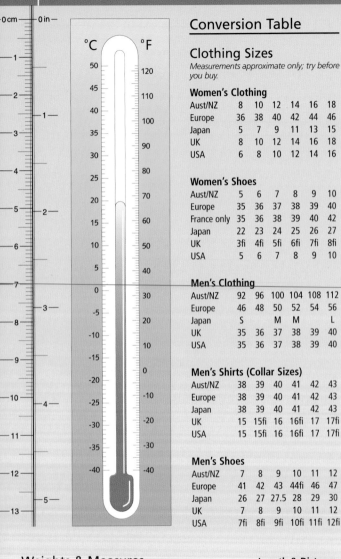

Weights & Measures

Weight
1kg = 2.2lb
1lb = 0.45kg
1g = 0.04oz
1oz = 28g

Volume
1 litre = 0.26 US gallons
1 US gallon = 3.8 litres
1 litre = 0.22 imperial gallons
1 imperial gallon = 4.55 litres

Length & Distance
1 inch = 2.54cm
1cm = 0.39 inches
1m = 3.3ft = 1.1yds
1ft = 0.3m
1km = 0.62 miles
1 mile = 1.6km

lonely planet

Lonely Planet is the world's most successful independent travel information company with offices in Australia, the US, UK and France. With a reputation for comprehensive, reliable travel information, Lonely Planet is a print and electronic publishing leader, with over 650 titles and 22 series catering for travelers' individual needs.

At Lonely Planet we believe that travelers can make a positive contribution to the countries they visit – if they respect their host communities and spend their money wisely. Since 1986 a percentage of the income from books has been donated to aid and human rights projects.

www.lonelyplanet.com

For news, views and free subscriptions to print and email newsletters, and a full list of LP titles, click on Lonely Planet's award-winning website.

On the Town

A romantic escape to Paris or a mad shopping dash through New York City, the locals' secret bars or a city's top attractions – whether you have 24 hours to kill or months to explore, Lonely Planet's On the Town products will give you the low-down.

Condensed guides are ideal pocket guides for when time is tight. Their quick-view maps, full-color layout and opinionated reviews help short-term visitors target the top sights and discover the very best eating, shopping and entertainment options a city has to offer.

For more in-depth coverage, **City guides** offer insight into a city's character and cultural background as well as providing broad coverage of where to eat, stay and play. **CitySync**, a digital guide for your handheld unit, allows you to reference stacks of opinionated, well-researched travel information. Portable and durable **City Maps** are perfect for locating those back-street bars or hard-to-find local haunts.

'Ideal for a generation of fast movers.'

– Gourmet Traveller on Condensed guides

Condensed Guides

- Amsterdam
- Athens
- Bangkok
- Barcelona
- Beijing (Sept 2003)
- Berlin (May 2003)
- Boston
- Chicago
- Dublin
- Florence (May 2003)
- Frankfurt
- Hong Kong
- Las Vegas
  (Sept 2003)
- London
- Los Angeles
- Madrid (March 2003)
- New Orleans
  (March 2003)
- New York City
- Paris
- Prague
- Rome
- San Francisco
- Singapore
- Sydney
- Tokyo
- Venice
- Washington, DC

index

See also separate indexes for Places to Eat (p. 126), Places to Stay (p. 127), Shops (p. 127) and Sights with map references (p. 128).

PLACES TO EAT

PLACES TO STAY

SHOPS

sights – quick index